Blossom

BLOSSOM

BLOSSOM

Abounding in God's Master Plan of Fruitfulness

Foreword by Dr. Myles Munroe

Olayinka Dada M.D.

Published by Dunamis Press
P.O. Box 337, Chester, NY 10918

Library of Congress Control Number: 2011946273
ISBN 13: 978-0-9822855-5-8
ISBN 10: 0-9822855-5-8

All the stories in this book are used by permission. To protect the privacy of those
who shared their stories with the author, some names and details have been changed.

Book Design by Leigh Anne Ference-Kaemmer
Front Cover Photograph by © Ying Feng Johansson | Dreamstime.com
Back Cover Photograph by © Fotografaw | Dreamstime.com
Inside Flap Photograph by © Olga Kovalenko | Dreamstime.com

Printed in the United States of America

To my son, Inioluwa Timothy, thanks be to God for making you the beginning of my blossoming.

To my lovely, pretty and admirable daughters, Oreoluwa Esther, Adeoluwa Mary-Favor and Opeoluwa Deborah-Peace; you all bring me so much joy and I love you.

CONTENTS

The wilderness and the
wasteland shall be glad for them,
And the desert shall rejoice
and blossom as the rose.

ISAIAH 35:1 NKJV

FOREWORD

This erudite, eloquent, and immensely thought-provoking work gets to the heart of the deepest passions and aspirations of the heart of all men- How to Blossom and become your best.

This is indispensable reading for anyone who wants to understand what it takes to blossom into the greatness you were created to be. This is a profound authoritative work which spans the wisdom of the ages and yet breaks new ground in its approach to understanding the keys to maximizing your God-given potential. This book will possibly become a classic in this and the next generation.

This exceptional work by Olayinka Dada is one of the most inspiring, practical, principle-centered approaches to this subject of becoming your best I have read in a long time. The author's approach to this timely issue brings a fresh breath of air that captivates the heart, engages the mind and inspires the spirit of the reader. The author's ability to leap over complicated theological and metaphysical jargon and reduce complex theories to simple practical principles that the least among us can understand is amazing.

Enjoy this book and let its pages of wisdom inspire you to blossom.

Dr. Myles Munroe
BFM International
Nassau, Bahamas

INTRODUCTION

I live in an area of divine magnificence; its beauty indescribable in the spring and summer months. The foliage comes alive and all kinds of animals and birds take their refuge in them. I believe as it is in the physical so it is in the spiritual. When God looks at His children, He expects to see His mighty hands and influence in them with unique and awesome outlook. The plans and purposes of God for His children are to blossom and to be a blessing to others around them.

WHAT DOES IT MEAN TO BLOSSOM?

In the dictionary, it means to develop or come to a promising stage. A person who has blossomed is a delight to behold. It means to grow into the limelight. Growth is a mystery and God will ensure we grow into the measure and fullness of the stature of Christ. Philippians 1:6 assures us that God will take us through the process of growth in His grace until He has completed His work. Luke 2:51 tells us Jesus grew physically, mentally, socially and spiritually. He grew in a holistic manner and as a result He could not be ignored.

Holistic growth is as a result of God's work in our lives. *A Christian who is blossoming* will come to a point where his or her life will burst out into an unceasing testimony like "I praise you because I am fearfully and wonderfully made; your works are wonderful, I know that full well" (Psalm 139:14).

To blossom means to flourish, to be successful or to prosper. God wants us to excel in all things. Joseph flourished in Potiphar's house. Daniel flourished in a strange land because the spirit of excellence was in him. Esther was elevated from her position as a slave to being a queen. It is never too late to excel in life. No dream is too late to realize. No condition is permanent; it is all in our mindset. Every human can be stretched to reach his or her goal no matter the color, status, position or age. John the beloved makes us understand the mind of God for our lives in 3 John 2:

> "Dear friend, I pray that you may enjoy good health and that all may go well with you, even as your soul is getting along well."

To blossom is to be evergreen. Psalm 1:3 says that when you are properly linked to the source of life, your leaves will always be green and not wither, everything you do shall prosper. This is an all round prosperity. You enjoy material, financial, medical, intellectual, mental, ministerial and social blessings. You are not boxed into any single state but have options available to you at all times.

To blossom is to bear fruit. The first commandment God gave man at the beginning in the Garden of Eden is to "be fruitful" (Genesis 1:28). It is the same commandment God gave Noah after the flood that destroyed the earth (Genesis 9:1). Fruitfulness is so important to God that He promises to evaluate us from time to time and any one that is not bearing fruit will be cut off (John 15:2). God wants us to bear spiritual fruits such as winning souls to expand His kingdom and fruits of the spirit as outlined in Galatians 5:22-23:

"But the fruit of the Spirit is love, joy, peace, forbearance, kindness, goodness, faithfulness, gentleness and self-control. Against such things there is no law."

Your transformation is not based on what you see or how people see you but what God sees in you. Some blossoming may be a change in your character or conduct or communication and in the fullness of time, it will appear to all.

To blossom is to operate in your season. A season is an appropriate time and Ecclesiastes 3:1 says: "There is a time for everything, and a season for every activity under the heavens." When God brings forth your season, all hosts of heaven and forces on earth are readily available to assist you. Everything and everyone cooperates with you. You are unstoppable, irresistible and you walk in the miraculous. In David's season, he experienced overflowing anointing even in the presence of his enemies (Psalm 23:5). His enemies could not stop him from rising up and enjoying God's best. In your season, you see the glory of God (Psalm 102:16); an uncommon increase, divine elevation, promotion, celebration and acknowledgement. Your status changes and you become a wonder to people.

Many months ago, a profound statement in the Bible changed my life. The statement was made when a young man's status was changed while operating in his season. It shows that it is possible to experience a major turnaround within a few minutes:

1 Samuel 10:11 NLT
"When those who knew Saul heard about it, they exclaimed, "What? Is even Saul a prophet? How did the son of Kish become a prophet?"

Obviously, Saul's folks noticed a positive difference in his life. They could not comprehend the sudden transformation and elevation. In biblical days, the band of prophets was prestigious and powerful. When your season comes, God lifts you up to a level where your deficiencies are compensated for by God Himself. When Esther, Joseph and Daniel operated in their seasons, nobody remembered they were foreigners. They all blossomed.

My patients often ask me if I have noticed a contradiction between science and spirituality. I do not blame them because as a physician I was trained in the Western medicine approach to life compared to Chinese medicine, eastern medicine or alternative medicine which most times is based on cultural, traditional or religious practices. Controversial debates between science and spirituality arise when inexplicable cases that defy medical and scientific knowledge, such as healing miracles, signs, and wonders manifest themselves. Hence, people struggle to believe in the power of God because we cannot see Him with our physical eyes and our senses have been trained to see something before we believe.

Some people with scientific and factual based thought patterns have a hard time wrapping their minds around the diverse world of religion and spirituality. A common example in our world is natural disasters. Hurricanes, tsunamis and earthquakes are very real and scientific. Sometimes thousands of people die from these events and in situations like these, some people ask: "If there is a God, why would He let that happen?" or "If there is a God, then why doesn't He help those people or do something about it?" I often say that because the world is limited in providing answers to world problems does not mean God is limited in taking care of the problems. The human brain is too small to analyze God. God is not stranded or confined to a specific way. It will go a long way if we do not look at issues only from the physical point of view, because not all sicknesses can be reasoned out and in such instances one should be able to look up to God for help since He is the Creator of the universe.

God cannot be examined in a science laboratory through a microscope or magnifying glass, but we can examine ourselves about our knowledge of God and if we look around us we will obviously find evidence of God's existence and intervention in the affairs of the world. Suffering is part of blossoming and we need to recognize the fact that opposition is inevitable. God works everything out that happens to us for our good. Romans 8:28 says "And we know that in all things God works for the good of those who love him, who have been called according to his purpose." God may be building some character in us by allowing us to go through suffering before blossoming.

This book is written to take you through the life of a blossoming Christian and the qualities seen in their lives. These qualities have been derived from the word Blossom:

B. Beauty of holiness
L. Lively and Longing faith
O. Overcomes obstacles
S. Sound Faith
S. Source minded
O. Outstanding exploits
M. Much fruits

I pray that you blossom in every situation.

BLOSSOM PRINCIPLES

1. Never lose hope in your journey to blossom.

2. It is God's will for us to blossom and be a blessing to others.

3. To blossom means to come to a promising stage and flourish.

4. To blossom, you have to be linked to the Source (God).

5. When you blossom, you are operating in the season God has for you and you become fruitful.

6. When you operate in your season, you experience the overflow God has for you and you become noticeable.

7. Always testify of God's goodness in your life.

8. Science cannot answer everything but God is all knowing and knows best for us.

9. The human brain is too small to analyze God. God is not stranded or confined to a specific way.

NOTES

Being filled with the fruits of righteousness,
which are by Jesus Christ,
unto the glory and praise of God.

PHILIPPIANS 1:11

JOURNEY
TO BLOSSOMING

L ife is a journey with an ultimate destination filled with major landmarks such as graduation from college or university, marriage, childbirth etc. The journey can be full of ups and downs but one needs to be focused and set one's gaze on the final destination.

I have a friend who is an avid rock climber. To get to the summit of every cliff and rock face, he endures hot weather, bruises and scratches from the complicated climbs. I asked him what exactly the appeal of this activity was, because it involved constant climb upwards regardless of painful challenges and frustrations. He told me that getting to the top (the ultimate destination of every rock climber) was worth it. To him, rock climbing is the same as living life. This is true because of insurmountable challenges and obstacles we inevitably face throughout our lives. Persevering to the top and appreciating the hard-earned fruits of his labor allow him to grow as an individual and never lose sight of the fact that his life has a definite, God-given purpose, no matter how much trying times and arduous setbacks may make him think otherwise.

Jesus never lost sight of where He was going and was able to overcome all the challenges in His path. Hebrews 12:2 says:

"fixing our eyes on Jesus, the pioneer and perfecter of faith. For the joy set before him he endured the cross, scorning its shame, and sat down at the right hand of the throne of God."

Not too long ago, Mabel and Ron came into my path of destiny. I saw something different in them in terms of their closeness to one another and comportment. They are humble and kind hearted with strong Christian values. They are a complete family and a unique couple and more so, with a goal of making heaven. I can confidently say they both complement one another to blossom as a flower. In my quest to find out what makes them different, Mabel shared her personal testimony with me and it confirms there is no glory without the Cross:

> *How could I have gone through so much and survived? There is only one explanation – by the Grace of God. 2 Corinthians 12:9 says: "My grace is sufficient for you, for my power is made perfect in weakness." His unconditional love for me is the reason I survived and I am here today to talk about it. By age seventeen, when I ran away from home for the last time, I had endured a sexual assault by two high school friends and one by several young men at a party. I also survived severe beatings at the hands of my mother. At age fifteen, I was placed in a foster home. I also won a local beauty pageant not long before I was placed in the foster home. I found it incomprehensible that a young girl like me could achieve straight A's in high school, have confidence enough to enter a beauty pageant but, at the same time, have to endure a horrendous home life. It has been very difficult to live with the stigma that comes with being a foster child. It is not something I have ever talked about openly to family, friends or colleagues.*
>
> *I was placed in a foster home because my mother beat me; not spanked, but beat me with objects I am embarrassed to talk about. I was beaten with an electrical cord, a piece of wood and a wire coat*

hanger. I went to school with welts and bruises on my body which my clothes covered. When the Children's Aid Society got involved I had climbed out of my bedroom window and went to a neighbor, who called my grandparents. My maternal grandparents were going to raise me before I was placed in a foster home. My parents caused so much trouble for them that the Children's Aid Society decided it would be best for me to be placed in a foster home far away from my hometown.

I returned home after about ten months because I missed my sisters and yes, I did miss my parents. My dad never beat me. My mom was married at 15 and had me just six months later. I believe she suffered a lot in her life too. The beatings did not start until I was about 14 years old. Before that, I had what I would consider a very happy childhood. I remember family picnics, birthday parties and Christmas. I am the oldest child of five girls and the only child beaten.

Life went well for me until 1988 when my world stopped, again. I was in a fatal car accident in which my mom was killed. My parents were visiting us with my little sister who is only two years older than my daughter. My mom and I had gone to a craft show that morning and we were on our way back to our house. I was driving and when I made a left turn, a pickup truck hit my car coming from the opposite direction. My head hit the steering wheel and I was knocked unconscious. It is my understanding that the car was on fire and a passer-by got a fire extinguisher from the Seven Eleven at the intersection and put it out. Both vehicles were declared "written-off." The fire department had to use "the jaws of life" to extract my mom from the vehicle. My mom passed away almost an hour later of extensive internal injuries.

I knew the exact second my mom died. I believe the Lord let me know. I was in my mom's room when a "Code Blue" was called. I was rushed out of the room. I was speaking with my husband and *father in the hallway when I felt this sensation go through my body from head to toe. I knew at that exact second my mom was gone. Then the ER doctor came out and told us. The seatbelt had cut my mom's windpipe and the blood drained into her lungs. She looked perfect from the outside but all the injuries were internal. Life as I knew it was over. I can't say I have gotten over that accident to this day. How I got through the following week was a miracle. Thank the Lord my aunts were there to hold me up, literally.*

The Lord spoke to me several times over the next few weeks. The night before my dad was to go to the funeral home I had a dream, which I believe was the Lord speaking to me because I was so overcome with grief and guilt. I was so afraid my mom was not saved when she passed away. I dreamt that her casket had to be "white as the driven snow" because she was pure. I called my dad the next morning and he fulfilled my request. I knew I had to say goodbye to my mom by myself and I wanted to tell her how sorry I was and ask her forgiveness. No one in my family has ever blamed me but the guilt and blame I put on myself was and is more than they could ever put on me. I was staying with an aunt and I told her I needed to go to the church alone before the service started. I cry even as I write this. My aunt called the minister and he opened the church for us. Mom's funeral was the last one held in this church and not a funeral home. It was the most difficult thing I ever had to do. I spent time alone with my mom and talked to her. I told her how sorry I was for taking her from her children and grandchildren. I asked for her forgiveness and then I kissed her goodbye. I am glad I did that now. It was painful and indescribable.

I spent seven years in therapy and one full month hospitalized. My psychiatrist had wanted to hospitalize me sooner but I would not agree to it. I finally agreed two years later. I must say that it was good for me. I was diagnosed with unresolved grief and physical and emotional exhaustion. I could not say the word "mother" or "mom" for years. When I first walked into the psychiatrist's office I told him I should be in jail because I had killed my mother. I had to come to terms with the fact that it was an accident. I thought I wasn't doing well and he told me that I actually was, which helped me a lot. He said I was a survivor, that some people would not even be where I was at that time. I was surprised by that. I only talked about the accident with him and no one else. My husband and daughter can tell you it was a taboo subject in our home for many years. It was ten years before I would talk about the accident.

I went back to school, completed grade 12 and then went on to college to earn a secretarial degree. Then I worked at a major bank where I earned the top award for service and excellence. I immersed myself in my work and achieved several awards and accolades. I was also honored by the mayor. I was on the Mayor's Honor List because I had fought City Hall to have the intersection re-designed where my accident happened. I went back to church and re-dedicated my life to God. It was in the church that I met my husband. After almost two years of marriage, we were blessed with our beautiful daughter

During all of these, I prayed and cried my heart out to the Lord many times. I begged for His mercy. I didn't know that He gave me His mercy and unconditional love all through the suffering. Psalm 103:8 says, "The Lord is compassionate and gracious." I thank God He was with me every step of the way because I would need him again to get me through a very difficult time. I continued working, living my life, raising our daughter and going to church and the devil tried once again to enter my life. I was diagnosed with Chronic Pain Syndrome and had to give up a job and profession that I loved. It was very difficult to accept. My life changed again. Years of pain and anguish did not turn me away from my Lord. I believe He gives us what He knows we can handle. Of course, I have asked the question why me?

In 2005, I needed God's mercy and love again when I went into *cardiogenic shock and was at death's door. I survived a 95% blockage in a main artery in my heart. The cardiologist said if my husband had not taken me to the hospital that night, I would have been dead in the morning. After spending several days in ICU and having a stent put in, I was released. I don't remember much about those first few days but I do remember seeing my husband and daughter at my bedside from above them and a voice told me I had to go back. And then, I remember a jolt as I hit my body. God's love and mercy has brought me through everything. He has never let me down. I never blamed the Father, Son or Holy Spirit for anything that has happened in my life. The Lord has always been there. The Holy Spirit has always filled me even when I thought my life was over. The Lord will use me as He sees fit. Everyone is tested, some more than others. I believe when I see the Lord He will tell me everything. I am blessed today to have four wonderful sisters, a loving daughter and husband of thirty years. I end with telling you this: God's mercy and love is great, greater than man can understand.*

Mabel's testimony is amazing – that someone could experience so much and still be a gem and radiating with joy. My advice for you as you take the journey to blossom is this: hope in God. I am talking about Jesus. Colossians 1:27 says "To them God has chosen to make known among the Gentiles the glorious riches of this mystery, which is Christ in you, the hope of glory." The journey may be full of twists and turns but if you fix your eyes on Jesus you will not be shaken or moved. When you hope in God, you look forward to your blossoming with desire and reasonable confidence. This means, you believe, desire, and trust God that all will end well. No matter the circumstance or situation we find ourselves, we know that God's plan for our blossoming will become a reality.

When the Lord sent a leader to deliver the Israelites from servitude, oppression, sorrow and bondage in Egypt, He promised to take them to a land that was full of milk and honey called Canaan. God's plan for His people was to bring them to a land where they would blossom and serve Him. The promise did not materialize in one day because they had to journey to the land. God desired that His people would hope in Him to take them to the land of promise. Their journeys were filled with many obstacles, inhibitions, dead ends and hindrances. In some situations, the outlook of things did not portray the promises of God concerning them. For example, when they got to the Red Sea which was a dead end to them from moving forward and the Egyptian army was pursuing them with their sophisticated weapons and armory, the people's hope shifted from the Lord of Lords and Lord of Hosts and they doubted God's power.

At the Red Sea, the Lord instructed Moses to let the people go forward. "And the LORD said to Moses, "Why are you crying out to me? Tell the Israelites to move on. Raise your staff and stretch out your hand over the sea to divide the water so that the Israelites can go through the sea on dry ground" (Exodus 14:15-16). The Egyptians and their horses were destroyed in the Red Sea while the Israelites walked on dry ground for safety. It is obvious according to Psalm 33:16-17 (NLT) that "The best-equipped army cannot save a king, nor is great strength enough to save a warrior. Don't count on your warhorse to give you victory- for all its strength, it cannot save you." God is the only One that cannot fail you in your hour of need because God is not a man that He should lie (Hebrews 6:18), grow weary or die.

Although there may be twists and turns on our road of life, the journey to blossom is continuous and should not be stopped, paralyzed with fear or preoccupied with fanfare. We must march forward irrespective of the barriers before us or the breakthroughs we have made. We need to keep focusing on the Lord until our journey is completed. God is consistent and His intentions never change. He is completely trustworthy. He is the Possessor of heaven and earth. The Lord's show of strength and power brought great celebration to the camp of Israel. Exodus 15:20-21 describes the mood of the people:

> "Then Miriam the prophet, Aaron's sister, took a timbrel in her hand, and all the women followed her, with timbrels and dancing. Miriam sang to them: "Sing to the LORD, for he is highly exalted. Both horse and driver he has hurled into the sea.""

Moses knew they were on a journey and refused to let the people dwell there and he led them away towards their blossoming land (Exodus 15:22). Many people lose hope in life due to disappointment, disease, depression, disaster, failure, delay, death of a loved one etc. Moses led the people from a point of victory into a wilderness and they wandered for three days without water. From scientific research, it has been found out according to the rule of survival skills known as The Rule of 3's that a human being has 3 minutes without AIR, 3 hours without SHELTER, 3 days without WATER and 3 weeks without FOOD. The Israelites ran wild because they had walked for three days without water and their hopes were definitely shattered. They had no more hope and when they got to Marah, they were disappointed (again) to learn that the water was bitter. Moses' hope in God was never shaken and he "cried out to the LORD, and the LORD showed him a piece of wood. He threw it into the water, and the water became fit to drink" (Exodus 15:25).

HOW TO HOPE IN GOD

Hold on to God's promises. There are lots of wonderful promises of blossoming in the Bible. We should hold on to these promises no matter how challenging things may be without wavering or doubting. A wonderful promise of God is in Psalm 92:12-14 which says:

> "The righteous will flourish like a palm tree, they will grow like a cedar of Lebanon; planted in the house of the LORD, they will flourish in the courts of our God. They will still bear fruit in old age, they will stay fresh and green."

In this Scripture, God is promising the righteous to blossom like a palm tree. Palm trees are strong, tall and very useful. This means the righteous will be fruitful, useful, relevant and strong. The Lebanon cedar can also grow very tall up to a height of about 130 feet. It is a symbol of strength, power and wealth. It is often used in building palaces and synagogues. God is promising the righteous to be strong, wealthy, stable and sound. Even in old age the righteous will still be virile, fresh and growing in grace. The promise may seem hard to fulfill but one needs to hope in God. Romans 8:24 says "For in this hope we were saved. But hope that is seen is no hope at all. Who hopes for what they already have?"

Have you located those promises concerning your blossoming?
When you find them, rely on them for God will bring them to pass.

Only believe God. The devil loves to contradict the promises of God and he comes subtly with words but one needs to make a sound decision to only believe the word of God. We hear many words today through philosophy, Internet, newspaper, radio, television and the list goes on. Abraham believed the word of God even though around him were words of lies and vanity. As a result of his unwavering obedience and belief, he was rewarded by God, as is written in Romans 4:18 "Against all hope, Abraham in hope believed and so became the father of many nations, just as it had been said to him, "So shall your offspring be."

Patiently wait on God. God's delay in fulfilling His promises or granting our requests does not mean denial. He is working things out on our behalf and ultimately for our own good. Hannah was a woman who patiently sought God year in and year out by going to Shiloh and in one year her patience paid off for the Lord remembered her (1 Samuel 1:19). She brought forth a child of destiny who became a renowned prophet in Israel. God obviously releases special blessings on His children who patiently wait on Him.

> Isaiah 40:31
> "But they that wait upon the LORD shall renew their strength; they shall mount up with wings as eagles; they shall run, and not be weary; and they shall walk, and not faint."

Those who wait on the Lord enjoy His very best. In Luke 1:5-6, Zechariah was a priest and married to Elizabeth from the descendant of Aaron. They were totally devoted, determined to please God with unwavering faith and lived with integrity. Despite serving God faithfully and God using them powerfully to impact lives, they carried a stigma of barrenness. Imagine God using you to solve other people's problems but yours remain unsolved. To compound their problem, they became old with grey hairs. However, they hoped in God because they were not perturbed by their circumstance. In Luke 1:8-15, the Lord fulfilled His promises by giving them a male child who was described by Jesus Christ as the greatest man born of a woman (Matthew 11:11).

The promise of blossoming is for every child of God and the choice is yours to get there or not. If you don't get there early, don't reason it out as if it is because of XYZ but continue to hope in God and commune with Him. Make a decision to know God more and long for Him constantly. Your knowledge of God should not be just one you call upon when you have a problem or someone you run to when the adversary is provoking a twist and turn in your journey to blossom. You must have a deeper and direct relationship with Him and this comes through prayer, worship and daily study of the Bible.

Like Zachariah, Elizabeth and other heroes of faith in the Bible, Daniel's story of how he survived the Lion's den and rose to a position of prominence in a strange land also proves that a consistent walk with God leads to a life of fruitfulness. To blossom consistently, one must trust in the Lord. Jeremiah 17:7-8 says, "Blessed is the one who trusts in the LORD, whose confidence is in him. They will be like a tree planted by the water that sends out its roots by the stream. It does not fear when heat comes; its leaves are always green. It has no worries in a year of drought and never fails to bear fruit."

Expect results. Our expectations should be centered on God and nothing else. This is the type of expectation God responds to. The Bible says in Proverbs 23:18: "For surely there is an end; and thine expectation shall not be cut off." The sick man at the pool of Bethesda in John 5 had expectations of healing and waited at the same spot for 38 years. The pool was stirred by an angel yearly and whoever got to the pool first was healed of any ailment. The sick man was there for thirty eight years despite being overtaken by other sick people to get into the pool. I applaud his great expectations, unlike people of today's generation who would have abandoned the spot to try other ways. We live in a fast paced world where we can microwave or drive through anything today. This mentality has eroded our waiting on the Lord.

BLOSSOM PRINCIPLES

1. Life is a journey requiring a set gaze on the final destination. Keep your focus on the Lord until the journey is completed.

2. On the journey to blossoming, hope in God. Believe, desire and trust that all will end well and that God's plan will come to reality.

3. God's plan is to bring people to a land where they will blossom and serve him.

4. Hold on to God's promises despite the challenges and road blocks.

5. The journey to blossom is an onward journey without being stopped or paralyzed by fear.

6. Only believe in God regardless of the enemy's subtle words which contradict God's promises.

7. Wait patiently on God because a delay does not signify a denial.

8. Expect results.

9. The promise to blossom is for every child of God and the choice is yours whether you get there or not.

10. Never lose hope in your journey to blossom.

NOTES

And your fame spread among the
nations on account of your beauty,
because the splendor I had given you
made your beauty perfect, declares
the Sovereign LORD.

EZEKIEL 16:14

2

BEAUTY OF HOLINESS

One of the striking qualities of a Christian who has blossomed is inner beauty. The Lord adds new colors that transform such a Christian. The plan of God at creation was to present a final product that could not be faulted. God achieved this because He beheld everything to be very good (Genesis 1:31). Even though man definitely lost some beauty in the Garden of Eden through disobedience, God is still beautifying His children. Isaiah declared this intent of God in Isaiah 61:3 saying: "to bestow on them a crown of beauty instead of ashes."

Ashes are ruins or remains after destruction or burning. They are worthless and often useless. God has the ability to exchange our ashes for beauty. Jesus came to turn our ashes into beauty. A mad man at Gadarene came in contact with Jesus and the result of the encounter was outstanding (Luke 8:26-39). He was possessed by devils for a long time and tormented to the point where he walked naked. He was ridiculed, shameless and with a big stigma - he had no covering. He could not be controlled by any man or professional. He probably made attempts to kill himself. There were no medications to calm him down and no mental institution to stabilize, monitor and observe him. He was living in tombs. His state represented a picture of a hopeless, helpless, useless, unclean, riff raff, of a man with no inhibition. He was stripped by the enemy and he had the kind of strength that could break chains and fetters. When he saw Jesus, the spirit in him cried out and fell down. It is interesting that evil spirits recognize the power of our Lord and worship Him. If the devil can do this, how much more can we who are in the light? We should humble ourselves and worship God in Spirit and in truth. God always dwells in the praises of His people. Our praise and worship should be centered on God the creator and not on His creation. Jesus asked for the name of the unclean spirit and it answered *Legion*, which means many. A Legion was a Roman military unit of 5000 to 6000 soldiers. Many evil spirits had entered this man to ravage him. We know this in John 10:10 which says "The thief does not come except to steal, and to kill, and to destroy.

The evil spirits pleaded with Jesus to throw them into the herd of pigs. The unclean spirits knew where to go and that is to unclean animals. Pigs are generally regarded as unclean animals in the Bible. The devil generally looks for unclean places to stay. He traces his way to where he can find any of his unclean properties. This is a lesson for us not to entertain any of the devil's unclean things. We should neither touch nor harbor or associate with unclean things. Although in the new dispensation, we should be careful in calling some people unclean but rather be in tune with the Holy Spirit and be ready to relate or reach out to anyone He places in our path. Peter almost missed the golden connection orchestrated by the Holy Spirit between the Jews and the Gentiles. We are all beneficiaries of his obedience today (Acts 10:28).

I reckon the owner of the herd of pigs must have experienced a nasty economic downturn as a result of the loss of the pigs. The one time mad man was transformed to a Christian gentleman; well dressed, calm, cool and seated at the feet of Jesus hearing the Word of God. When the people caught sight of him, it was an unimaginable situation. They stood in awe of Jesus and became afraid of Him. No situation or circumstance is impossible if God's Word is available. The Lord added colors and beauty to his life. He had a new beauty that men could not ignore. His shame was received and his nakedness covered. He was given a fresh start and commissioned to blossom for the Lord of Lords.

Luke 8:38-39
"The man from whom the demons had gone out begged to go with him, but Jesus sent him away, saying, "Return home and tell how much God has done for you." So the man went away and told all over town how much Jesus had done for him."

Jesus cast out all the legion of evil spirits by His words. His words are still powerful today. His words have the ability to change situations instantly. Psalm 107:20 says: "He sent out his word and healed them; he rescued them from the grave." He magnifies His words more than His name (Psalm 138:2) and His words still clean today (John 15:3). All that you need for your deliverance, healing, success, beauty, promotion is a word from the Lord. Peter was wise to yield to His words because His words have the ability to create from nothing.

Peter said in Luke 5:5: "Master, we've worked hard all night and haven't caught anything. But because you say so, I will let down the nets." The same Word that added value to the world that was formless and empty in the beginning brought tons of fish to the same spot Peter launched his net in the deep of water; "And this time their nets were so full of fish they began to tear!" (Luke 5:6 NLT) Peter and his company of fishermen with their experiences and accolades in fishing gave in to His word, and after their own futile attempts, they experienced a mighty harvest. God's words have the ability to comfort, sharpen, restore, encourage, build, lift up, empower, enlighten and so on.

A young college student came in contact with His Words through our ministry and her destiny was restored. She had made up her mind to close God from her heart but God's Words reached her where no one else could reach. In her own account, she said:

> *Growing up as a pastor's daughter, I felt like my father cared more about the church than he cared about my sisters and I. With this at the back of my mind, I wasn't interested in growing spiritually because I thought that the closer you get to God, the farther apart you get from the people around you and I did not want that to be my case. I have always been very lazy with an "I couldn't care less" attitude. I continuously make plans in my head but I never actually do any of these things out of laziness. I also give up easily. At the slightest sign of impossibility or failure, I give up and have a convincing excuse. I think this has been a major setback for me. One Sunday morning, the pastor made a call and I went forward. As he laid his hand on me and prayed, I felt a surge of energy go through me and I could not stand any longer. Immediately I fell on the floor and I heard God speak to me. He said "Don't waste your life, if you do, I will take it away from you" and I felt something go for my heart. He also said "If you waste your life, when the enemy comes, I would have no reason to spare you". This was a life changing wake up call for me.*

This young student experienced a definite transformation at the hands of God. Her experience was a catalyst that allowed her entire life to transition to the state of blossoming. She is now enjoying a Christian life and bearing fruits in the Kingdom. Her story tells us that no one is beyond God's rescue and deliverance. God can give beauty to a willing heart. Zechariah and Elizabeth received their children of destiny in their old age. The Lord removed their rags of shame and replaced them with His beauty. Their joy knew no bounds and made Elizabeth to retreat to a place of gratitude to God.

BLOSSOM PRINCIPLES

1. God adds beauty to the life of every Christian.

2. Praise God always and recognize the power of God.

3. Don't entertain or harbor any of the devil's properties.

4. The Word of God is powerful and it dissipates all impossibilities.

5. The Word of God cleanses.

6. God can rescue and deliver anyone.

7. Always be in tune with the Holy Spirit for direction.

8. After God cleanses, He gives a fresh start.

NOTES

Those that be planted in the house
of the LORD shall flourish in the
courts of our God.

PSALM 92:13

3

LIVELY AND LONGING FAITH

In high school, my classmate Barry was afflicted with a form of *Muscular Dystrophy*, a debilitating disease that causes the progressive weakness of skeletal muscle tissue which hampers locomotion and general movement. Barry was confined to a wheelchair because his legs could no longer support his weight. To the delight of his teachers and classmates, despite his incapacitated condition, Barry proved to be a very smart, quick-witted, lively, and good-humored student. Although well-liked and admired by majority of the school population, many people wondered about his future, especially as graduation approached. They asked, "What would he do after high school? How would he pursue his dreams? Would he stay home and depend on his family to take care of him for the rest of his life?"

Surprisingly, Barry did not worry about his future. Throughout his life, he had faith that he would be fine and that he would pursue his dreams regardless of his less-than-ideal physical circumstances. "In a wheelchair, but can laugh and love," was a phrase he often used to describe himself. With this determined attitude infusing all aspects of his existence, Barry successfully graduated from university and is currently pursuing a career as a comedian. Now, he does what he loves: making people laugh with his infectious sense of humor and in the process, brightening and touching other people's lives along the way.

A lively and longing faith is realized only in the heart of those who have a dream and a burning desire to demonstrate this liveliness both in the body and in spirit. To be lively is to be full of energy and vitality; to be healthy and effervescent. A lively person often says 'I am knocking on wood.' Whenever I treat sick people I appreciate our loving God and His tender mercies. Good health is a gift from God and He deserves our praise and gratitude.

In biblical days, we read about the Hebrew women's great health. This was at a time a new king came to power after Joseph and his brethren had died. In Joseph's era, the Israelites enjoyed great favor in Egypt because Joseph was the Prime Minister. They hid under Joseph's shadow and rode on the back of his influence. The death of Joseph and his generation brought a turning point and a new era began. In this new era, they were not accepted and forced into a life of servitude. Despite the subjugation of their oppressors and afflictions from their taskmasters, the Lord still blessed them.

> Exodus 1:12
> "But the more they were oppressed, the more they multiplied and spread; so the Egyptians came to dread the Israelites."

They multiplied to a level and their enemies wanted to eliminate them. The king of Egypt issued a decree that all their newborn sons should be killed and their midwives were given the authority to carry out this task. The midwives spared the Hebrew children because they feared God and when confronted by the king of Egypt, they responded in Exodus 1:19 saying: "Hebrew women are not like Egyptian women; they are vigorous and give birth before the midwives arrive." I believe the testimony of the midwives was that the Hebrew women were strong, healthy and experienced no difficulty or delay in child bearing. It is fair to say that the Israelites blossomed in the land.

My father in the Lord, Pastor Enoch Adeboye sometimes says: 'to understand the meaning of a *word*, one should look critically at its opposite.' The opposite of *lively* is weakly or frailty or sickly. This example is portrayed in the woman who had the issue of blood for twelve years (Luke 8:41-48). To have bled non-stop daily for so long tells me she must have lost a lot of blood. She was probably anemic, weak, powerless, inactive, frail, cachetic, lonely and languishing in poverty. This biblical woman had tried many physicians and had spent all her earnings to no avail. She must have traveled many places to seek a solution. It is interesting to say that gynecological surgery may not have been available during that period. Her sickness defied a medical solution. This must have made her depressed, sorrowful and shameful. She carried a stigma that made her avoid public places. She was forbidden from public places and mingling with people as it is written in Leviticus 15:19-23 (MSG)

> "When a woman has a discharge of blood, the impurity of her menstrual period lasts seven days. Anyone who touches her is unclean until evening. Everything on which she lies or sits during her period is unclean. Anyone who touches her bed or anything on which she sits must wash his clothes and bathe in water; he remains unclean until evening."

Based on this knowledge, all the people would have avoided her. This woman was spiritually alert and could sense the power of the Master. She was determined to get closer to Jesus irrespective of her condition and the risk of walking around multitudes of people with her issue of blood. She conceived wholeness in her heart. She had a dream of a new life that is possible with an encounter with Jesus. She desired to be lively and to blossom. She conceived a change of status and purposed to touch the hem of Jesus' garment.

To stop the source of her issue of blood, she reached out by faith to draw power from the Source of power, Jesus Christ. She received her miracle and was healed instantly (Luke 8:44). Her life took a 180 degree turn. She had previously gone in the direction of death but now, in the direction of life. She did what had never been recorded before and got an uncommon blessing. She became lively and experienced new vigor and vitality. Her miracle confirms that consistent and committed faith in the Lord does not go unrewarded.

Her determination was similar to Elisha's when his master Elijah was to be taken away. Elisha was discouraged by the sons of the prophet and even his master told him to stay behind but he was resolute in his effort to receive a double portion of Elijah's anointing. Elisha could as well be distracted with the fanfare of the chariot that took Elijah away but he fixed his gaze on Elijah as instructed by him in order to have his heart's desire.

> 2 Kings 2:10-12
> "You have asked a difficult thing," Elijah said, "yet if you see me when I am taken from you, it will be yours, otherwise, it will not." As they were walking along and talking together, suddenly a chariot of fire and horses of fire appeared and separated the two of them, and Elijah went up to heaven in a whirlwind. Elisha saw this and cried out, "My father! My father! The chariots and horsemen of Israel!" And Elisha saw him no more. Then he took hold of his garment and tore it in two.'"

The journey to the lady's deliverance began when Jesus responded to Jairus' clarion call to heal his sick daughter. On the way to Jairus' house, a lot of people followed Jesus. Among the people were likely to be spectators who wanted to watch the healing power of the Lord. There were speculators who were interested in hearing the news of the day and ready to spread it everywhere; bread disciples who were mainly interested in being physically fed for the day and serious-minded people, who followed Jesus to receive miracles, Word of life and eternal life.

Lack of focus can hinder your miracle. God expects us to be focused on Him like a laser beam (Hebrews 12:2). Jesus Himself knew those who followed Him because of what they would receive from Him for He said in John 6:26 "Jesus answered them: "Very truly I tell you, you are looking for me, not because you saw the signs I performed but because you ate the loaves and had your fill."

The physical state of the woman with the issue of blood reminds me of a lady I heard about in South Africa with anemia (a decrease in the number of red blood cells). Her red blood cells were dangerously low. Such people are usually described as being "paper white". She was in anemic heart failure, frail, weak and dying. All that was needed to save her life was a blood transfusion but she refused due to her religious beliefs. This belief was further strengthened by her husband and religious group. The medical team told the elders of her church and her husband to allow her receive the blood transfusion but they refused and she eventually died.

Not too long ago, Ruth shared her testimony recently about how she overcame her own issue of blood and her ordeal brought the biblical story alive:

I had an issue of blood for four years termed hypermenorrhea and menorrhagia. It began after I got married. I expected the issue to be resolved especially in this part of the developed world but to my utmost surprise and disappointment, I was told by a consultant gynecologist that he had not seen this type of prolonged uterine bleeding before in his years of practice. Immediately I thought of the woman with the issue of blood in the Bible. I took three different types of medication but none of them worked. I was later taken to the operating room for the lining of my womb to be scraped to see if that would stop the bleeding. That didn't work. I was later told by a consultant that if I went to the operating room again, it would be life-threatening and a second opinion was needed. At that point I believed all was lost.

I gave up my faith in the Lord and immediately accepted what the doctors had said. I assured myself that the doctors would still find a solution. The medical condition affected my husband and I in many ways. We had to replace our mattress because the old one was soaked with blood. We stopped visiting people and stopped going on holidays to avoid embarrassment. It was not easy because each time we went; we had to take a bag of beddings to use so I would not stain their bed sheets. In situations where we ended up (unavoidably) visiting people, after our hosts went to sleep, my husband would go into our car to bring out our own beddings and very early in the morning we would quickly put them back in the car. Furthermore, when we went for church holiday, I slept on the hotel bedroom floor with my husband to not stain their mattress because that month the bleeding was like a fountain. We made a decision that night not to go on holidays again especially because we experienced a very terrible body ache.

The vaginal bleeding was quite severe that I was restricted to some particular clothing. Whenever I stood up in public places, my husband would quickly check my dress. It became an ordeal to visit places or survive the day at work because I was in and out of the bathroom several times. I was later transferred to another doctor and she decided to take me off all medications because they did not work. She concluded that if the blood could stop then she could refer me for In Vitro Fertilization (IVF). Instantly my hubby rejected it and said 'IF GOD CAN STOP THE BLOOD, HE CAN GIVE A CHILD.' The doctor agreed and asked me to serve the God my husband serves. She was notably surprised that he was the one encouraging me to hold on to God because in her experience, the wife was often the one that demonstrated stronger faith.

On the way home we argued and when we got home, I read the story of the woman with the issue of blood again and my faith began to pick up. My husband always prayed to God to take His time in giving us a child but I did not say amen to such prayers. I only prayed to God to stop the bleeding and not to give us a child at the time. One thing we both agreed on was to have a girl first and when I began this experience, my husband would put a baby girl`s cloth on the bed and at night he would put a sleep suit. When leaving the bedroom, he would take the cloth to the living room and put it on the chair. He obviously called things that were not as though they were. He even gave me the list of names for our baby. He always called me by the child`s name even when he knew things were not working and he was not having sexual intercourse with me because of the condition.

When Daddy Adeboye came to our city, I expected a word of knowledge concerning my case but that didn't come. I was also unable to see him. When he left, my husband was still having the meeting with the ushers' team. He advised that since it was not possible to have the General Overseer pray for me, I should attempt to sit on the chair which he used during the program. I called him from the front that there were too many people waiting to sit but my husband persisted and suggested that I touch the handle of the chair and I did. I recollected that the woman in the Bible only touched so I touched my stomach and told God that by this time the following year I would carry my baby girl. I didn't remember to say 'amen' so I wasn't really sure if the prayer went anywhere. The blood flow stopped instantly and when I got home, I checked and didn't see anything.

On Monday, I went to the doctor and she said she would quickly refer me for the IVF but my husband insisted we would not do it. He used the opportunity to get close to me and I became pregnant. When I checked the home pregnancy kit, I didn't believe it so I took it to the pharmacy and they explained it to me that I was pregnant. The doctor conducted more tests on me and immediately referred me to the early pregnancy department for a scan. Throughout my pregnancy, there was no pain, no morning sickness, and no complications. I gave birth to the most beautiful baby girl in the world. When I was infertile and having issues of blood, friends and family did not know about it, so they only prayed for a child for us. The main thing we did while going through this wilderness was that we made ourselves happy. My husband was very supportive; stood by me and made me happy. He was not irritated at all. I thank God for his life.

BLOSSOM PRINCIPLES

1. In our contemporary world, God continues to give good health.

2. A great way to appreciate our loving God for good health is to attend to sick people.

3. Our focus on God should be like a laser beam.

4. Your situation should not determine your altitude.

5. In the face of discomfort, difficulties and prolonged hardship, unwavering faith in the power of Jesus Christ will always lead to breakthrough.

6. Determination is one of the necessary and indispensable qualities required when believing in God to act concerning a situation.

The testing of your faith produces perseverance.
Let perseverance finish its work so that you may be
mature and complete, not lacking anything.

JAMES 1:3-4

4

A BLOSSOMING
CHRISTIAN WILL
OVERCOME OBSTACLES

Nestor, a graphic designer living in Guatemala, migrated to Canada hoping to find success in the animation or video gaming industry. Although he was slightly nervous about moving to a foreign country, he decided to go anyway to make a name for himself and to improve the living conditions of his family. Upon his arrival, he soon realized that finding and securing employment in North America was not easy. For example, many potential employers who interviewed him did not acknowledge the degrees and certifications he obtained in Guatemala. They preferred candidates who were educated and trained at "recognized" institutions. His immense disappointment with the employment situation made Nestor rethink his faith.

He began praying every day to God for guidance on what he ought to do. Setting aside his own personal ambitions, Nestor's desire to help his loved ones was essentially what convinced him to stay in Canada and weather the storms of uncertainty. He eventually realized that because he was just starting out, he should not be too picky about the job opportunities that came his way. He kept reminding himself that meeting his life goals would take time, patience, and an unwavering trust in God. One month after he migrated to Canada, he was hired as a technical support agent for a call center. Although the job did not pay as much as a career in graphic design would, Nestor was glad and thankful for the steady income and of course, the opportunity to provide for his family.

Within two years, and with plenty of hard work, Nestor had not only helped his family move to a better place to live, but he had also saved enough money to start upgrading his graphic design certifications at a local community college. To this day, Nestor firmly believes that God enabled him to endure the hardships of settling in Canada in order to help him rethink his unrealistic ambitions in life and focus first on caring for those who love and support him.

We live in a competitive world and it has become the survival of the fittest. A Christian who is blossoming will learn to overcome tough situations (1 John 5:4), rejection, hindrances, oppression, accusation and afflictions. It is often said there is no gain without pain. A Christian who is blossoming needs to overcome storms. A storm is an unplanned, unexpected and unannounced life event that may stop us from advancing or receiving our miracles. A storm is an obstacle; a barrier that hinders or destabilizes. A storm is a sudden change in what we consider to be normal. Storms are inevitable; no matter where you live or who you are, you will face storms like sickness, failure, temptations, separation from loved ones, financial loss, and unemployment.

In Mark 6:45-56, Jesus called His disciples and instructed them to go to the other side. The other side was the land called Gennesaret, where Jesus and His disciples were celebrated, honored and their influences were unquestionable. The expertise of Jesus was highly sought and the people took maximum advantage of it. People were receptive of Christ's ministry there and the disciples experienced real power and demonstration of God's healing miracles. There were abundant of miracles, healings, deliverance and blessings. "As soon as they got out of the boat, people recognized Jesus. They ran throughout that whole region and carried the sick on mats to wherever they heard he was. And wherever he went, into villages, towns or countryside, they placed the sick in the marketplaces. They begged him to let them touch even the edge of his cloak, and all who touched it were healed."

The fact that Jesus and his disciples could practice their ministry freely and in such a welcoming environment demonstrates the power of living a life that is blossoming. This is enjoyable when you operate in the midst of people who recognize and celebrate the gifts of God in you. To get to this other side of life is difficult and full of obstacles. For example, while the disciples were on their way to Gennesaret, the devil saw the future and brought storms their way. Storms come at the verge of your breakthrough. When the devil sees our glorious tomorrow, he fights us tooth and nail to accomplish his purpose.

THE ENEMY BRINGS STORMS INTO OUR LIVES TO:

* **S**ink our boat so that we don't arrive in our destiny.

* **T**ear us apart. Many have been shaken by storms and torn apart from loved ones, families and friends. Hopes have been shattered and some left wounded.

* **O**verwhelm us; to stress and burn us out and make us focus on the raging storm instead of the great God.

* **R**ender us restless; making us wander from place to place in search of solutions and tagging people wanderers instead of wonders to their community.

* **M**ake us afraid and lose our belief in God.

* **S**eparate us from God. This is the ultimate goal of the enemy. He wants people in his camp. If you are not in God's camp, you have no other choice but to be in the devil's camp.

Paul was a Christian who blossomed and one of his secrets is revealed in Romans 8:35-39. Paul was convinced beyond any reasonable doubt that nothing could separate him from the love of God. He made up his mind to remain and trust God always. He learned that storms don't last forever and if Christ is in our boat, no storm can capsize our boat or shipwreck our faith. Sometimes it may look like the Lord is sleeping in our boat, but no storm can separate us from God. We don't need to fear or be overwhelmed by the magnitude of the earthquake. What matters is that God created all and has the ability to control all of His creation.

However, not all storms come from the devil. Some are as a result of our disobedience while some may be permitted by our loving God to:

- **S**how that God is the Master Controller of the whole universe.
- **T**urn our attention to God.
- **O**pen our eyes to the greatness and influence of our God.
- **R**elease us from any form of bondage.
- **M**ake us perfect in the Lord and wanting nothing.
- **S**ave us from impending danger or disaster.

In the book of Jonah, God told Jonah to go and preach in Nineveh so that the people could be turned from their wickedness. Jonah thought he could run away from God's presence and assignment; and he took a ship to Tarshish. Jonah forgot that God is omnipresent (Psalm 139:7-13) and no man can run away from His presence. After Jonah had paid the fare, boarded the ship and started sailing, the Lord showed He is in control of the affairs of the world. "Then the LORD sent a great wind on the sea, and such a violent storm arose that the ship threatened to break up" (Jonah 1:4). This storm was permitted by the Lord not to sink the ship or tear apart the people but to change the direction of Jonah's destiny, turn his attention and draw him to God. This purpose was fulfilled because the sailors threw Jonah into the sea and he was swallowed by a whale and then vomited on dry ground three days later (Jonah 1:5-17). In the end, all the sailors and Jonah were saved from impending danger or disaster; even the people of Nineveh were eventually saved from destruction. Jonah later blossomed in the land of Nineveh but only after overcoming the storms in his life. May you too overcome in Jesus name.

BLOSSOM PRINCIPLES

1. Not all storms come from the devil. We may be the architect of our own storms through disobedience or carelessness.

2. The enemy will bring storms in your journey to blossom.

3. Storms surface at the verge of your breakthrough.

4. Storms are simply distractions to remove your sight from the saving God.

5. Be resolute in your faith in God during the times of storms.

6. God can use storms to get our attention and draw us closer to Him.

7. Blossoming Christians have a story behind their glory.

NOTES

And without faith it is impossible to please God, because anyone who comes to him must believe that he exists and that he rewards those who earnestly seek him.

HEBREWS 11:6

5

SOUND FAITH
IS A MARK OF A
BLOSSOMING CHRISTIAN

I remember Eric as the elderly Deacon at the church my family and I attended when I was growing up. As I approached my teenage years and started to prepare for my role in the church's youth ministry, I began to talk more often with him about developing my skills as a prayer leader in my congregation. I was particularly keen to improve my public speaking skills, since I had always been a shy, nervous, and socially anxious student at school, the kind who, out of fear of scrutiny and ridicule from my peers, never volunteered an answer or an opinion unless directly and specifically prompted by the teacher.

Deacon Eric, I thought, was the best person to ask for advice on this matter because he already had years of public speaking experience. Thankfully, my hunch proved right. He told me the importance of maintaining eye contact with my audience and projecting my voice across the room. He also taught me that allowing the strength and solidity of my faith in God to manifest themselves through my comportment would certainly be an inspiration to the members of our congregation, both young and old. He shared an inspirational story about his own journey.

Before he became a Deacon, he had severe difficulties speaking in front of the congregation because he had a speech disorder which made him stutter frequently. Compounding this already daunting challenge were the accompanying self-conscious assumptions he formulated in his mind; for example, that his audience either laughed at or completely misunderstood his words.

Deacon Eric even recalled the numerous times he would break out in a cold, frenzied sweat at the mere thought of facing a captive audience at a public speaking venue in church. What turned him around and enabled him to conquer his speech disorder and resultant anxieties for good was the realization that for God to employ him as an instrument for His work, he must, through his actions as well as his words, demonstrate the fortitude of his faith in the Almighty. What Deacon Eric taught me was this: for one to preach about the strength and security that can be found only in the Lord, one must demonstrate that very strength and security at work in one's own life.

A sound Christian is strong, reliable, financially secure and competent. Such a person remains stable, sturdy, steady and solid regardless of setbacks in life. His or her life blossoms when this kind of strength and security become assets to a person even in the face of danger. Psalm 82:1 says that God stands in the congregation of the mighty. God does not pitch tent with the wimp, whiner or one wallowing in a pity-party. God prepares us for the time of our blossoming. All the people who blossomed in the Bible were first prepared by God through life circumstances. Moses trained in the school of Egypt for forty years; then in the wilderness school for forty years before being called at the age of eighty. Moses was sound in every area and the Lord attested to His unique character in Numbers 12:5-8 (CEV):

"I, the LORD, speak to prophets in visions and dreams. But my servant Moses is the leader of my people. He sees me face to face, and everything I say to him is perfectly clear. You have no right to criticize my servant Moses."

Soundness also means to be relevant. When you are relevant, you command presence as well as the attention of those around you. Joseph rose to prominence in a strange land. The king of Egypt so empowered him that he had great influence in the land. "Pharaoh told Joseph, "I am Pharaoh, but no one in Egypt will make a single move without your stamp of approval" (Genesis 41:44 MSG).

Soundness also means to be firm and solid in one's beliefs no matter the negative situation or circumstance. The devil loves to torment with fears. The devil makes false evidence to appear real. Fear is a big weapon the enemy uses and fear is the dark room where the devil develops people's negatives. He then presents these negatives as his report but a sound believer holds on to the report of God and not the report of the devil. God has not given us a spirit of fear, but of power and of love and of a sound mind.

A testimony was shared in our church of God's intervention and healing by a resounding young man. His faith in God during his ordeal is worthy of emulation:

"It was a Monday morning, sometime in early April 2011, I woke up feeling feverish, and I thought it was just flu. I had not been sick in 20 years I recalled, but the pain grew worse. After about 4 days, I called Dr. Dada who is also my dear pastor in Hamilton. He carried out tests, prayed for me and then referred me for more tests at Saint Joseph Hospital. The situation puzzled doctors for days but after several medical tests and close monitoring the discovery

was made. "You have Endocarditis," the doctor said. "Endo what?" I thought. I had never heard of it. "What is that?" I asked. In my heart I knew that the name of Jesus Christ is greater than all names.

Infective endocarditis means infection of the inner lining (endo) of the heart (Card). This infection is usually caused by deadly microorganisms that go into the inner layer of the heart valves and cause inflammation (-itis). Since the hearts function is to pump blood to the rest of the body, infection of the heart could affect the other parts of the body. The symptoms of infective endocarditis include fever, chills, generalized weakness and loss of appetite. These symptoms are present because your immune system is trying to fight this infection that is hidden in the heart valves. This heart disease also causes vegetations in the heart valve that lead to abnormal heart sounds (murmurs). If left prolonged for a long time, this disease could lead to heart failure and ultimately death.

Honestly, I felt a little scared. Many thoughts crossed my mind, while I pondered on several outcomes and questions, for every negative thought I muscled up a positive counter answer from God's word. I believe that Faith calls those things that are not as though they were so I declared by Faith; "I shall live and not die to declare the Glory of the Lord in Land of the living. It's only the beginning of greater things to come. By the stripes of Jesus Christ, I am healed. God is just creating a new heart in me".

I received a lot of encouragement and love from church members, family, friends and pastors and this rejuvenated my strength and the will power to live again. The kind words and prayers gave me hope and helped me to believe that this was just a passing phase, all things will work together for my good, that my pain will pave the way for deeper passion for God and further authenticate His existence in my life. While on the hospital bed, weak and undulating pain, I looked forward to sharing my testimony of healing. I saw myself telling

> *everyone of how I once was down but now I am healed though I was still in pain. The joy, love and support I received at the time assured me that there was more to live for, I remember God's word that He will never leave nor forsake me. I refused to feel sad rather I was glad and thank God today, I AM COMPLETELY HEALED. Glory to God!*

Moses was given the task of leading the Israelites to the Promised Land and sent twelve spies to the land of Canaan. Ten brought back reports and said they could not conquer the land because the men were hefty, strong, mighty and many. Joshua and Caleb made a different confession that they would conquer the land with God on their side. In Numbers 14:1-5 the rest of the people believed the majority. They murmured, complained and grumbled. Grumblers are faithless; they always see their Goliath as an intimidating factor instead of seeing a big God. David saw Goliath as too big to miss or not see.

We need the power of God always. Without it, we cannot be sound and blossom. Jesus told His apostles, stay, don't do ministry, until you receive God's power. Acts 1:8 (NKJV) says "But you shall receive power when the Holy Spirit has come upon you; and you shall be witnesses to Me in Jerusalem, and in all Judea and Samaria, and to the end of the earth." Without this power, you will run dry and burn out. By the grace of God, the Bible says on the day of Pentecost, the power came upon the early apostles. It transformed Peter's fear to courage and Thomas' doubt to faith.

Jesus also empowered His disciples and they were able to overcome the fear of the unknown, failure and rejection (Luke 9:1-6). Jesus sent them to preach the kingdom of God and to heal the sick. To carry out this assignment they needed to overcome their fears and be sound in all aspect. The reasons for their success included the following:

They were connected to Jesus and operated under His authority.

Jesus gave the disciples authority; He gave them a covering. Authority is vital and keeps us in check and confers special power on those who have it. That is why a cop can stop you anytime and you will obey him because he has been given authority by the government. If you do not obey, he can shoot. In a case in Alberta, Canada, a police officer shot and killed a man that supposedly carried a gun but it was later found out that the guy was carrying a fake gun.

So the question is: *by what authority do you do what you do? Do you have the authority of God in your life?* Without authority, the devil will make a mess of your ministry. We need the power of God to overcome all the challenges in this environment and not to be stripped naked. The seven sons of Sceva operated without the authority of Jesus (Acts 19:13-15) and the devil told them: "Jesus I know, Paul I know but who are you?" They were chased by the demons they were casting out and stripped naked. They lacked power and authority.

They were obedient.

Jesus instructed them to take nothing for their journey. That was a tough instruction. Take nothing for your journey, don't even take money, don't take food, don't take anything, just go, and they went. Abraham became father of many nations because of his obedience. God just looked at him and said 'come, I will take you to a new place, a new city,' and God did not tell him where he was taking him. God just said follow me and he obeyed. Even when God gave him the instruction in Genesis 22:2 to "Take your son, your only son, whom you love—Isaac—and go to the region of Moriah. Sacrifice him there as a burnt offering on a mountain I will show you." Abraham still obeyed.

Absolute obedience produces great surprises. A parishioner shared this interesting testimony:

> *I was in a healing conference and the person ministering to us called the spiritual leaders and laid hands on us and said you can do everything through the power of our Master. Then he called people for healing. It happened that somebody came my way for prayer. Seeing this person approaching, I suddenly felt inadequate and said to myself, "How can I do this? Why can't this person just ask for prayer from someone else?" I shivered and did not know that I had the power in me. I asked the person what the problem was and he communicated that he couldn't hear. I didn't believe that God could use me to heal another until it happened.*

❋ They were prepared by Jesus for opposition.

Luke 9:5 says "If people do not welcome you, leave their town and shake the dust off your feet as a testimony against them." This means that as they were preparing, even under authority, some people would still reject them because they rejected Jesus Christ. God prepared their minds for battle and opposition from men and government. He instructed them to not fight back but shake off the dust from their feet. Today, I see Christians saying, "Look, we are in the 21st century, if you fight me, I will also remove my shirt and strike back."

In studying the Mosaic commandments, Jesus raised the bar on the same old ones (Matthew 5:17). They look so simple, but they are actually tougher than Mosaic laws. Moses gave them a bill of divorce. He said don't commit fornication and adultery (the real act), like the woman that was caught in the real act (John 8:4). However, Jesus said that if you look at a woman wrongly, you have committed adultery or fornication. Jesus said if a man slaps you on one cheek, turn the other one. He said people will oppose you and question your authority. People will reject you and lie against you. There will be strife, there will be envy, there will be jealousy and the list continues, but Jesus said, don't fight them. I am talking about physical fight. You can fight people spiritually; you can go on your knees and pray, but don't fight them physically because it will bring disrepute to the Gospel (Luke 10:10-12).

The disciples had to totally rely on God for everything because they had nothing. Some Christians today don't believe in doing this, because we currently live in an age where the government provides for its citizens. For example, if you come to this land without a cent, you can be automatically guaranteed accommodation and some money in your pocket. The attitude that "the government will always take care of me" discourages many people today from relying on God for their well-being. But God is saying there must be a total reliance on Him, not on man, and not on the government. We must not place our faith and trust on a system, but should instead place them on God. Today we face the challenge of having an army of God that wants everything even before they enlist.

✸ They had great faith in God.

Looking at the Scriptures, faith is what determines how far you can go because faith is the currency of the kingdom. The substance of things hoped for, the evidence of things not seen. It says by faith the elders were justified. Faith is so crucial for this kingdom walk that if you don't have faith, you can't go far. Hebrews 11:6 says without faith, no man can please God and those that come to God must first of all know that He exists. It is by faith that you are a Christian. The disciples had great faith. They were sent on a fresh journey.

I remember when we were coming to Hamilton from Newfoundland, people said: "Hamilton? Don't go there" but we came and we fell in love with it, and this is our Rehoboth today. You need to have faith in God and not what people say. Faith in God is absolute trust in God. The disciples had faith that God would supply all their needs according to His riches in glory by Christ Jesus. They did not look back and when He sent them out two by two, they went.

God gives responsibility before ability and it is faith that will make you tap into that ability. God just sent them out and they did not know that they could do it. Remember, they were always hiding under the shadow of Jesus Christ. Jesus now said, 'Okay you step out. This is your responsibility. This is what you should do' and they needed faith to actually withdraw that potential from heaven. Faith is needed to receive power from God and to conquer fear. The disciples came back with great joy as a result of their success.

Another Biblical example is Habakkuk. Habakkuk was a prophet who was full of complaints; and almost thirty complaints were recorded in his book. His attitude changed from complaints to rejoicing at the end of the book. He wrote one of the most beautiful songs in the Scriptures in Habakkuk 3:17-19:

> "Though the fig tree does not bud and there are no grapes on the vines, though the olive crop fails and the fields produce no food, though there are no sheep in the pen and no cattle in the stalls, yet I will rejoice in the LORD, I will be joyful in God my Savior. The Sovereign LORD is my strength; he makes my feet like the feet of a deer, he enables me to tread on the heights."

Habakkuk describes a situation where he wakes up one morning and there are no clothes in his closet, no food in the kitchen, no car to drive, no friends to associate with, no strength and no work for him to do. In this case, he says he would never complain or grumble or whine but rather praise God. A sound Christian is vocal in his or her praise, rejoices and gives God thanks in all situations.

BLOSSOM PRINCIPLES

1. God is still in the healing business today if only you can have faith in Him.

2. Fear is the opposite of faith and can prevent you from taking positive steps.

3. The power of God makes you sound in all areas of your life and eliminates fear.

4. Absolute obedience is a prerequisite for receiving the wonderful power of God.

5. Operating under the authority of God allows you to be connected to God's power.

6. Faith is a heavenly currency that helps you to connect to the power of God.

7. Faith is a God-pleasing tactic and a fear-destroying strategy.

8. Faith helps you to stay firm despite the situations or challenges you will face in life.

NOTES

I am the vine; you are the branches.
If you remain in me and I in you,
you will bear much fruit;
apart from me you can do nothing.

JOHN 15:5

6

A BLOSSOMING CHRISTIAN IS SOURCE MINDED

My childhood friends and I built a tree house behind the barn on my parents' farmland. We would always go to this tree house to escape the rest of the world; to enjoy one another's company, and help maintain something we could all call our own. To our minds, the tree house was both a shelter from the literal and figurative storms in our youthful existence, as well as a companion that provided us with shade and protection from the sun. I have many fond memories of the time spent in that living shelter. Not long after my sister and I graduated from college and left our home country, my father passed away after a brief battle with illness. Broken-hearted and unable to continue living in the same place without her husband of almost fifty years, my mother sold the farm and moved to another town.

After I graduated from college, I nostalgically decided to visit my childhood home and, of course, the tree house upon which I had spent the better part of my teen years daydreaming about my plans for the future. What I assumed would always remain fertile land had now become another casualty of urban sprawl. The farm my parents cultivated had now given way to the gutted makings of a new subdivision. The barn my father built had been razed to the ground and the modest planks and ropes that made up the platforms of our tree house were nowhere to be seen. Surrounded by pieces of construction equipment that were likely responsible for ruining the landscape of the surrounding area, the tree itself was now effectively cut off from its ecosystem and life-giving natural resources. Though still alive, the tree that once provided refuge to me and my friends now stood as a weathered, old, and dying remnant of days gone by. The main roots of the tree have been severed leaving barely none to connect it to the nutrients from the ground.

A tree cannot blossom without its roots connected to the source of life and nutrients, so also is a Christian. To blossom as a Christian, one needs to be grafted and connected to the Vine (John 15:1-2). If we remain in Him, we have no reason to fear. He further said in John 15:4-5: "Remain in me, as I also remain in you. No branch can bear fruit by itself; it must remain in the vine. Neither can you bear fruit unless you remain in me. I am the vine; you are the branches. If you remain in me and I in you, you will bear much fruit; apart from me you can do nothing." To connect to the Source (God) is to have absolute trust in His power. You release your entire life to Him.

When you put your confidence in God, you are like a tree with roots linked to a stream of water where it saps food. This tree will never drop its leaves but will always experience green leaves and blossom. Any Christian who loses connection with the Source will stagnate and experience futility. Peter tried it in John 21. He was selected by Jesus and told to stop fishing for fish and start fishing for men. Peter was included in Jesus' inner circle. He was among the three disciples Jesus committed the leadership of the church. He was at the mount of transfiguration where he experienced the glory of God first hand (Matthew 17). Jesus prayed for him especially so that his faith would not fail him.

After Jesus was raised from the dead, Peter was to put things in order with the help of God but he decided to take matters into his own hands. He went fishing and misled the rest of the disciples. He went back to his former trade and trusted in his own abilities to excel but failed woefully. "I'm going out to fish," Simon Peter told them, and they said, "We'll go with you." So they went out and got into the boat, but that night they caught nothing" (John 21:3). The Master came to his rescue and made him realize the need to commit his life and all to God. Peter obeyed and the result was amazing. Nebuchadnezzar was also an example of a man who tried to succeed alone without any form of connection to God. He constructed the hanging garden of Babylon and other technological feats were erected during his tenure as king of the Neo-Babylonian Empire. He woke up one day and started bragging about the nation he had built with his own power and might. This self-exaltation reached heaven and God responded with His greatness accordingly.

Daniel 4:28-32
"All this happened to King Nebuchadnezzar. Twelve months later, as the king was walking on the roof of the royal palace of Babylon, he said, "Is not this the great Babylon I have built as the royal residence, by my mighty power and for the glory of my majesty?" Even as the words were on his lips, a voice came from heaven, "This is what is decreed for you, King Nebuchadnezzar: Your royal authority has been taken from you. You will be driven away from people and will live with the wild animals; you will eat grass like the ox. Seven times will pass by for you until you acknowledge that the Most High is sovereign over all kingdoms on earth and gives them to anyone he wishes."

The king wandered in the forest for seven years and the experience taught him a lesson to humble himself. He looked to God and confessed Him as the Controller of the Universe. He was reconnected to His Source and was totally restored (Daniel 4:33-37). In the journey to blossom, remember that a stream that forgets its source will dry up. The same applies to anyone who forgets his or her source. Jesus illustrated this profoundly in his parable in Luke 12:16-21(MSG):

> "The farm of a certain rich man produced a terrific crop. He talked to himself: 'What can I do? My barn isn't big enough for this harvest.' Then he said, 'Here's what I'll do: I'll tear down my barns and build bigger ones. Then I'll gather in all my grain and goods, and I'll say to myself, Self, you've done well! You've got it made and can now retire. Take it easy and have the time of your life!' "Just then God showed up and said, 'Fool! Tonight you die. And your barnful of goods - who gets it?' "That's what happens when you fill your barn with Self and not with God."

I presume the rich man thought his hard work had yielded the great harvest. What a wrong assumption this man had! He forgot that the mystery of growth is not known to every farmer. A corn of wheat must first die before it can live. God has input in every planted corn that shoots up above the ground and brings forth the desirable harvest (John 12:24).

LESSONS FROM THE PARABLE OF THE RICH MAN

1. **Not all blossoming or riches come from the Lord.** Just because a man is prospering does not mean that man is connected to his Source. The devil also reaches out to his people but his riches are uncertain and do not last forever. If you are rich without God, you are nothing. This man invested in earthly things and invested poorly towards God. He definitely misplaced his priorities on earth. God can not commit true riches on people who misplace their priorities. Matthew 6:33 says: "But seek first the kingdom of God and His righteousness, and all these things shall be added to you."

2. **Not all rich people are wise.** We live in a world where we celebrate wealth, status and influence. Some celebrities and wealthy people are idolized and people seek their views on things happening around the world. Some can't offer wisdom because they are not connected to the ancient of days. It is obvious that this man in the parable did not consult God in decision making. When faced with the dilemma of how to manage his riches, he did not look to God for direction or rely on Him. He was proud and was eventually brought down.

> Psalm 20:7-8 (MSG)
> "See those people polishing their chariots, and those others grooming their horses? But we're making garlands for God our God. The chariots will rust, those horses pull up lame - and we'll be on our feet, standing tall."

77

3. **Selfishness does not lead to increase in God's equation.**
All he thought about was how to increase himself and he
forgot God and his neighbors. He felt he had reached a point
in his life where he did not need God. What an ignorant man!
He lacked knowledge of the power and greatness of our God.
Psalm 62:11 says, "One thing God has spoken, two things I
have heard: Power belongs to you, God." The Psalmist also
declared the greatness of God in Psalm 104:24, "How many are
your works, LORD! In wisdom you made them all; the earth is
full of your creatures." He was very selfish and individualistic.

The average person is selfish and this is because the world
erroneously teaches us that it is in withholding that we are
safe. We are told that what we keep in the bank guarantees
for our future. In my opinion, this man did not remember to
pay his tithes or think of bringing special offerings to God
in gratitude for his bountiful harvest. He did not even have
plans for people around him. He only thought of expanding his
barns. He was called a fool because he did not factor God into
his thinking (Psalm 14:1). He had no relationship with God.
He did not have a link with his Maker. He felt safe and secure
in his apparent riches. The Scriptures teach us that what we
release to God and others is what is safe.

> Proverbs 11:24-25
> "One person gives freely, yet gains even more; another
> withholds unduly, but comes to poverty. A generous
> person will prosper; whoever refreshes others will be
> refreshed."

4. **God's factor cannot be ignored in your fruitfulness.** God's intent for man at creation was to multiply and increase him. God has a hand in every increase in your life and that is why He must be acknowledged at all times. A Christian who has blossomed is always connected to God. When you are plugged in, your heart must be established to maintain connection to God (James 5:8). This involves constant appraisal of one's relationship with God. Philippians 2:12 says: "Therefore, my dear friends, as you have always obeyed, not only in my presence, but now much more in my absence, continue to work out your salvation with fear and trembling."

To avoid power interruption, we must connect to the Source continuously; at all times and not sporadically. Avoid anything or anyone that short-circuits the connection. When you plug in to God, you should expect distractions from the devil. The devil is in the business of roaming around and looking for one to steal and destroy. One needs to watch and pray just like Jesus prayed for Peter in Luke 22:31-32 saying: "Simon, Simon, Satan has asked to sift all of you as wheat. But I have prayed for you, Simon, that your faith may not fail. And when you have turned back, strengthen your brothers."

COMMON DISTRACTIONS
BY THE ENEMY

How do these negative forces operate? These opposing forces operate through the following three ways. Though these three are not exhaustive but are the common ways the enemy uses to disrupt our connection with the Source.

(a) **Planting tares.** This makes the conductor impure and sap energy. With tares, the flow of God's spirit and power in your life is reduced. This why we must be vigilant to prevent pollution from the enemy. Matthew 13:25 says: "While everyone was sleeping, his enemy came and sowed weeds among the wheat, and went away." The devil will resist you but you have to know how to fight. Nehemiah had a dream of rebuilding the broken walls of Jerusalem in a strange land. He was faced with Sanballat the Horonite, Tobiah the servant, the Ammonite and Geshem the Arabian (Nehemiah 2:19). He contended with the forces, overcame and eventually completed the repairs of the walls of Jerusalem.

(b) **Disobedience to instruction.** The enemy makes us discard God's instructions. Most electrical devices are sold with the manufacturer's manual which gives clear direction and instructions. If the instructions are not followed, the equipment will not function properly. One day, a friend visited me from Africa and he needed to use his medical equipment. It did not work because the voltage was different from the one used in North America. In a similar vein, to be rightly connected to God and subsequently blossom, we need to obey God's instructions as written in His manual (the Holy Bible).

(c) **Pride.** This creates a disconnect from God. Pride makes one pompous and arrogant. A proud man is like low voltage equipment connected to a high voltage power supply and the end result is damaged equipment. The Bible says pride goes before destruction (Proverbs 16:18) and James 4:6 says: "God opposes the proud but shows favor to the humble."

A Christian who has blossomed does not forget his or her Source; gives honor and adoration to God; ascribes all glory and power to Him; desires to know Him more and rests in Him.

BLOSSOM PRINCIPLES

1. Every Christian must have their roots connected to God.

2. Anyone who decides to not connect and those who lose their connection with God, will deteriorate progressively due to lack of nutrients.

3. Taking all the credit for blossoming and giving none to God (the Source) comes with accompanying punishment.

4. When you blossom, God expects you to share your fruits with others and not be self-centered.

5. Being connected to the Source is not a one-time thing, it is a continuous process.

6. Be on the lookout for the devil's tactics and counter them with prayer.

7. Obedience is key in staying connected to God. Read God's Word, discover His instructions and obey accordingly.

8. God has a zero tolerance policy towards pride. As you blossom, don't let pride set in because pride leads to destruction.

NOTES

Those who do wickedly against the
covenant he shall corrupt with flattery;
but the people who know their
God shall be strong,
and carry out *great exploits*.

DANIEL 11:32 NKJV

7

A BLOSSOMING SOUL HAS OUTSTANDING TESTIMONIES

There is a lilac shrub that grows in my backyard. During the spring season, sometime between May and June, this lilac shrub abundantly produces beautiful, light purple blooms that catch the eye of every guest who visits my garden. What especially stands out about this stunning plant over and above the other colorful flowers in my garden is that it also releases an aromatic fragrance that carries for quite a distance. Encountering a lilac plant in bloom is certainly an exhilarating and memorable experience. Its vibrant green foliage is beautiful throughout the spring and summer months and it is really when the plant is in full blossom that one can truly appreciate it. This is a testimony of the beauty and wonder of God's creation.

A blossoming Christian stands out from his or her peers. This will be evident all around the person. Nancy's testimony touched me greatly about God's mighty move in her life and family. Her triumph of faith brought her outstanding exploits and her testimony is unique indeed. It shows indeed what Daniel said in Daniel 11:32 that "those who do wickedly against the covenant he shall corrupt with flattery; but the people who know their God shall be strong, and carry out great exploits."

My dad's younger sister raised me from the age of seven after my dad died, till I was eighteen. There was a misunderstanding and my sister came and took me away from my aunt's house to live with her. I found out that my menstrual period stopped just one month after leaving aunt's house. It could have been a coincidence, but my sister did not think so. She wanted to go and confront my aunt but her husband who is a pastor stopped her. He said to leave the situation to God and just pray about it.

I got born again two years after this problem began and I attended a lot of prayer and deliverance sessions. My menstrual flow was very irregular. It would disappear for years, show up once, and disappear again. I saw many gynecologists in Nigeria and I was placed on pills which I took daily that helped restore the flow. I did not like the burden of the pills, so I stopped taking them and my period stopped. The years leading to marriage were tough ones. Three men came into my life and professed their desire to marry me, but left after they heard my issues with menstruation. Nevertheless, the man that God had made for me did not run. He married me when I was twenty-eight, and at this time, there was no solution to this problem.

I moved to England to be with my husband and we continued to seek medical help. We saw a consultant about three times a year for three years and a lot of tests were conducted. At the end of the three years, I was told that I was undergoing early menopause. The consultant explained the condition with a diagram and he said that unlike the normal woman who had numerous eggs, I had none. He said that even if we decided to go for In Vitro Fertilization (IVF), I would need to find another woman to donate her eggs. He mentioned that I should expect to feel pain and some things to my bones as well as the other parts of my body during this process. Finally, he said that nothing could be done about it medically.

This was the time when we had no choice but to totally let go, relax and trust God. I went for a service in Nigeria known as the Holy Ghost Night, and Daddy Adeboye said that there was someone out there whose menstruation period had stopped and whoever the person was will be healed. I claimed that prophecy for myself, and I changed my prayer. I stopped praying for God to restore my menstrual flow and started praying that God should give me a child. My husband was amazing the whole time and he was very instrumental in keeping my faith up. He would always prophesy on my womb every morning and even ask me about the children in my womb when he got back from work. My situation did not move him during this trying time in our marriage.

God also encouraged me vividly through His Words and Messages from men of God. During a service some time ago, He talked to me and reminded me of how excited I would be if the Queen of England said she would do something for me. Even if I had not received it yet, I would still tell everyone because I know that the Queen is able to do whatever she says she will do. Then God said: "How much more Me?" After that, I went out and gave a testimony about how God had answered my prayers even when I had not seen the evidence yet. The people around me including my husband thought I was pregnant, but I explained that it was just an act of faith. A year later, in 2005, I got pregnant and I could not believe it. I had to take tests after tests to convince myself that I was actually pregnant. This happened without my menstruation cycle coming back. God bypassed that law, took me to the next level and our son was born in 2006.

In Luke 7:36-50, a woman of questionable reputation anointed Jesus and the crowd around the area who knew the history of the woman felt embarrassed. It was a private dinner for Jesus and this woman got to know that Jesus was in town and came there without an invitation. She lived a reckless life, carried a huge stigma and was probably lonely because her sinful state was known to her community. This woman came with a mission and that was to humbly serve and honor Jesus Christ before His death.

Luke 7:36-38
"When one of the Pharisees invited Jesus to have dinner with him, he went to the Pharisee's house and reclined at the table. A woman in that town who lived a sinful life learned that Jesus was eating at the Pharisee's house, so she came there with an alabaster jar of perfume. As she stood behind him at his feet weeping, she began to wet his feet with her tears. Then she wiped them with her hair, kissed them and poured perfume on them."

She brought an expensive perfume in an alabaster box. She washed Jesus' feet with her tears and hair. To understand her depth of service and humility, we should remember that in those days even though they had footwear they were not like fancy shoes we wear today. This woman knelt down at Jesus' dusty feet and wept producing profuse tears on His feet. She later regained her emotion and composure, and then she wiped His feet with her hair and kissed His feet. She poured the expensive perfume on Jesus' feet. This is an example of true service. She showed that true service involves sacrifice which involves giving up our pride, rights, ego, time, dignity and risking our necks to do the work of God. She gave her all to the Master. She took her time to clean His feet with her hair and gave her treasure - an expensive perfume.

The disciples recognized the worth of the perfume and some said: "Why this waste of perfume?" (Mark 14:4) Despite her sacrifice, she was condemned and men used her past to judge her present

(Luke 7:40). Jesus saw her remarkable and extraordinary service. She trusted the Word and the performance that the Word brings.

Jesus drew Peter's attention to her service and sacrifice by saying she was motivated because she knew her sins were forgiven.

> Luke 7:47-50 (MSG):
> "If the forgiveness is minimal, the gratitude is minimal." Then he spoke to her: "I forgive your sins." That set the dinner guests talking behind his back: "Who does he think he is, forgiving sins!" He ignored them and said to the woman, "Your faith has saved you. Go in peace."

Jesus saw the woman as a deep thinker who felt her forgiveness was huge and her thankfulness to God should be extraordinary as well. She gave by revelation. She understood that the timing of Jesus' death was near and decided to anoint Him. This act made her gift timely. The women that came to the tomb of Jesus on the third day came late with their spices. Their offering was not at the right time because they could not find the body of Jesus because He had risen (Matthew 28:1-3). She became a very outstanding disciple to the extent that Jesus defended her service and declared that any where the gospel is preached, her story of service will not be omitted (Mark 14:6-9).

MEDIOCRITY DOESN'T CATCH GOD'S ATTENTION

The exploits and services that caused God to move were carried out in ways that had never been heard of before. These giants of faith didn't just decide on the spur of the moment to do exploits for God. There were well laid out plans, careful consideration and a lot of deep thinking involved. Consider the service King Solomon rendered in Gibeon as recorded in 1 Kings 3:4-14. This was one of the most outstanding services given to God in the Bible. First, he chose to offer the sacrifice to God in Gibeon because it was known in those times as the "most important high place" (1 Kings 3:4). King Solomon was so well invested in giving God a service that was beyond excellence that he put a lot of thought into the content and even the location of his offering to God.

When you consider the magnitude of what Solomon did, you will see that someone who does not love God cannot offer this kind of service to Him. Let me paint a simple picture to bring home the gravity of what this wise king did. One thousand burnt offerings can be equated to one thousand animals and remember, only the high priest could offer sacrifices to God those days. Imagine the time invested by the high priest in sacrificing one thousand burnt offerings on one altar, the stamina and determination of Solomon to go through with it even when weariness and tiredness crept in.

After this great act of service was rendered, God did not even wait one day, but appeared to Solomon that same night (1 Kings 3:5) ready to release whatever blessings he desired because God's attention had been captured. God gave Solomon more than he asked for and today, we celebrate him as the wisest man that ever lived. History was made. Solomon and his household blossomed. They enjoyed the rewards of his outstanding exploits on that altar in Gibeon. Stories of outstanding exploits of people ahead of us can be a catalyst in our own journey to blossoming. The stories of the Bible were written for our examples. I perceive that Solomon learnt how to give uncommon offerings to God through his father's legacy. David decided to give God a sacrificial offering to stop the plague through the angel of destruction that came on his people as a result of his sin. David purposed to not give to God anything that did not cost him something (2 Samuel 24:24). David must have heard about how

God honored the sacrificial offering of Abel (Genesis 4) and Father Abraham (Genesis 22).

One of the talented youths I have come across in ministry shared his testimony of how God used another man's testimony to help him focus on his studies. He said:

> *I met a young man who worked in an oil company during my industrial training. He started off well at a prestigious university He knew God and was very principled until partying instead of studying got to him. He loved fame and was really passive about his Cumulative Grade Point Average (GPA). In his final year, life dawned on him and he felt a great heaviness. He was very concerned about his future because he knew that his current GPA couldn't take him to graduate school. He studied hard but still did not get results. He didn't know how he was going to do it but he needed marks close to perfect to redeem his GPA level. After attending a church service (something he had stopped doing for a long time), he felt a great conviction to do things the right way. He became a Christian and went back to his principled way of living. At the end of his final year, he redeemed his GPA. In fact, he did very well. His testimony pushed me to do well in my fourth year at the university.*

"HOW MANY TIMES CAN I TESTIFY?"

A blossoming person can never testify enough. Ince, an international student in our church experienced the mighty touch of God and he started to blossom in his school. He became an ardent soul winner for Christ and at the same time he started experiencing uncommon blessings from God. God started moving people from all over the world to be a blessing to him. As he was blessed, he would testify in the church. One evening he called me and asked in a serious tone:

"Pastor, how many times can I testify about God's faithfulness in my life?" I asked him to explain the reason for his question. He replied that he had been put down by one of his mates and teased that he is testifying too much. I advised him accordingly to keep giving God the glory and not allow the devil to have the last word over him. Today, this young student is shining for Christ.

> Revelations 12:11
> "They triumphed over him by the blood of the Lamb and by the word of their testimony; they did not love their lives so much as to shrink from death."

TO BE IN THE BLOSSOMING SEASON IS TO ALWAYS HAVE A SONG IN YOUR HEART

My friend Bob is in his late fifties and everyday he sings scores of praises to God. One day, he shared his experiences with me and I could not but glorify God too. His upbringing was very modest and God raised him from a lowly state to a height he never dreamt of in life. He was written off by his family and friends because of his nonchalant attitude to life. He was a drunk and a lover of women who found it difficult to pay attention to his studies. When his season came, he finished his studies though at an advanced age and got a good job. God blessed him tremendously and his home could not contain the wealth. He is very excited about the goodness of God in his life and vocal in his praise in the secret or open places.

Not too long ago, I received this powerful testimony from a friend who is in the blossoming season:

Before I started practicing as an obstetrician, I was told by my friends and family members in very clear terms that it was impossible to combine being a pastor's wife, mother and doctor. My husband and I discussed it and we were convinced that practicing medicine was a mandate from God. I trusted God all the way because when he sends you on an errand, He equips you with everything you need to accomplish the task. I stood on this Scripture: "God is able to make all grace abound to you..." It was a daily event to ask for grace for each day and God supplied it. When things became tough and it seemed like it was not going to happen, I asked for more grace and each obstacle gave way, one after the other.

I completed my training in record time and excelled in my exams. The next challenge was to combine all that I had learnt in my spiritual journey, my family and social life and my career. I remember the saying that "he who has a head has no cap and he who has a cap is headless" and I kept asking God "is it not possible to have both a head and a cap?" The answer to that was "With man, it may be impossible but with God, all things are possible."

Things were very tough when I started work as an obstetrician. I was so busy I thought I was going to slump one day. I was expecting our third child, was on call up to three times a week and sometimes performed up to six caesarean sections in one day. At the end of the first term of my contract, I convinced myself that I didn't want to practice clinical medicine anymore, so I did a master's degree in public health and it was a full time program.

At the end of all the rigors of going through another line of training, I had to work as a clinician for another two years. I did this because the available jobs in public health would take me away from my husband and young children. It was a matter of priority for my family and I to be together. Again, I convinced myself that practicing medicine was not for me. To lose my family to the stress of work was not an option. I became a home maker, was there for our four lovely children (the oldest was fifteen and the youngest, two) and my husband sorted out the financial aspects of our life by himself. It was at this point we moved from South Africa to Canada.

I was determined to be the most contented homemaker the world had ever seen; practicing medicine would be part of my life story and that would be it. I was not ready to read for any more exams or cross any other hurdle to practice medicine in another country. I had already done it twice outside my home country where I trained (you don't want to be in my shoes). Before we left for Canada, God told us without doubt, this was going to be a place for our restoration. We didn't understand what that meant but we went anyway.

Today, I am practicing obstetrics and gynecology at my pleasure. My house is approximately two minutes' walk from the hospital where I work. This really helps me with managing my time at home, clinic and hospital. My public health training certainly did not go to waste because it has actually given me the necessary skills needed to manage my clinic. God has provided businesses and outstanding ministry opportunities for us which my husband manages. God has blessed us with a lovely and supportive church family beyond our imagination. Our first two daughters are in the university very close to home. They love God and are fulfilled doing what they do. Our last two children are in the elementary school which is about a minute's drive from home and work. I am on call at weekends only if I want to. I go out of town to preach or shop if I have to. I am a servant of God, a wife, a mother and an obstetrician & gynecologist. I did not give up one role for the other. I am a living witness of this fact: "He has given us all things that pertain to life and godliness." I appreciate God's faithfulness all the way.

My friend's story is a living testament to the importance of believing that God can lead us to the heights of fulfillment in life if we trust in Him to balance all aspects of our life for His glory. Her family is an example of how God leads us to a state of blossoming.

BLOSSOM PRINCIPLES

1. The word "outstanding" is used to describe something exceptional; a blossoming Christian should have exploits that are just that.

2. Pure unpretentious service that is beyond excellence is what Jesus expects from us.

3. An outstanding service is devoid of pride, rights, dignity, ego and cowardice.

4. God's worth exceeds whatever outstanding means to you.

5. Outstanding services and exploits are born out of complete gratitude to God and are poured out without reservation.

6. Exploits for God are amazing when outstanding meets divine timing.

7. Outstanding service will be foremost in the heart of those who witness it and will be passed along to posterity long after the steward is gone.

NOTES

He shall be like a tree planted
by the rivers of water,
That brings forth its fruit in its season,
Whose leaf also shall not wither;
And whatever he does shall prosper.

PSALM 1:3 NKJV

8

A BLOSSOMING CHRISTIAN BEARS MUCH FRUIT

Ever since I have known Antoinette, a woman who lives in my neighborhood, she has always wanted to have a child. She and Dennis, her husband, have been trying to start a family for years, but with no success. During the course of their twenty-year marriage, they consulted several fertility specialists; spent plenty of time and money travelling to different clinics and hospitals which provided them only with the faintest hope of having a child. This overwhelming feeling of despair started to take its toll on their relationship and at one point, built up resentment between husband and wife. Their marriage was on the verge of a break up. They both renewed their commitment to God and moved closer to God, and it wasn't until the couple submitted to God's plan and trusted Him to decide whether or not they were to have a baby, that Antoinette, at the age of fifty, became pregnant and gave birth to the couple's first child, a healthy baby boy named Andre.

Fruitfulness is important to our Creator. He has created us to bear fruit and be relevant in our land. In the Bible, we see patriarchs of faith who bore fruit in their old age. Abraham and Sarah had their child of promise, Isaac in their old age. Elizabeth and Zechariah also had their child of destiny, John in their old age. It is never late for a child of God to fulfill God's commandment of fruitfulness. We know a tree by its fruit so also a child of God is known by the fruit he or she bears.

We can bear many fruits as a child of God. We can bear the fruit of the Spirit (love, joy, peace, forbearance, kindness, goodness, faithfulness, gentleness and self-control) as highlighted by Paul in Galatians 5:22-23. Paul also admonished his protégé, Timothy, to set an example for the believers in speech, in conduct, in love, in faith and in purity (1 Timothy 4:12). God is more interested in building our character than our charisma. Paul encouraged Timothy to build his character for it will stand the test of time. As a result of our character, the rest of the world will be able to see the presence of Jesus in our lives and this will serve as an attractive force that pulls them to the kingdom.

In today's world, people learn about Christianity and how to live as a Christian not by buying Bibles alone, but by seeing Christianity at work in our daily existence. Our words should build up and not tear down; bless and not curse. A Christian should not be known for foul language (Ephesians 4:29). God expects us to be ardent soul winners. We should draw as many as possible to the kingdom of God. This takes a lot of effort on our part and we need to sacrifice our talent, time and treasures to bring many people to the kingdom of God. Paul said necessity is placed on Him to preach the gospel and highlighted in 2 Corinthians 12:15 (NLT) " I will gladly spend myself and all I have for you, even though it seems that the more I love you, the less you love me." Jesus gave us a parable on the importance of fruitfulness in Luke 13:6-9 saying:

"A man had a fig tree growing in his vineyard, and he went to look for fruit on it but did not find any. So he said to the man who took care of the vineyard, 'For three years now I've been coming to look for fruit on this fig tree and haven't found any. Cut it down! Why should it use up the soil?' "'Sir,' the man replied, 'leave it alone for one more year, and I'll dig around it and fertilize it. If it bears fruit next year, fine! If not, then cut it down.'"

FRUITFULNESS IN THE KINGDOM AND LESSONS FROM THE PARABLE

❋ **God expects fruitfulness** and demands it from His children. He expects returns on His great investment on man. We have no option but to be fruitful in the account of God. This is because out of all of His creation, God has invested so much in man. Man was made in the image of God and empowered to do exploits. God blessed man and empowered him to prosper, reproduce, fill the earth and take charge of everything (Genesis 1:28). To whom much is given, much is expected. Fruitfulness brings glory to God. He is pleased and delighted with our returns. "When you bear (produce) much fruit, My Father is honored and glorified, and you show and prove yourselves to be true followers of Mine" (John 15:8 AMP).

❋ **God has a timetable for us** and expects us to bear fruit in his time frame. Ecclesiastes 3:1 says "There is a time for everything, and a season for every activity under the heavens." He will knock on our door at His own time because He has a calendar for us and we cannot see His schedule. He alone knows the best time to act and holds us accountable. No one can alter His time table. He knows when to show up and demand for fruitfulness. God expects us to use our gifts and influence lives for Him.

✤ **Unfruitfulness disappoints God** and He does not joke with it. God can get tired of unfruitfulness and can abandon or even cut off the person from the kingdom. Unfruitfulness is a curse. God cursed Saul's daughter (Michal) with fruitlessness for insulting David after he danced extravagantly before God (2 Samuel 6:20-23). God pronounced a curse of fruitlessness on anyone that disobeys Him (Deuteronomy 28). Jesus also placed a curse on the fig tree for its fruitlessness (Matthew 21:18-20). Unfruitfulness is undesirable in God's kingdom.

1. **God sees an unfruitful Christian as wasting His resources** and taking up unnecessary space. Many are occupying positions and enjoying special privileges but without performing. Such an unprofitable Christian is denying others of God's riches and resources. I call them Barr body leaders or ministers, meaning, dormant and unprofitable children of God. Such leaders fold their arms, refuse to develop themselves and as a result become inactive.

2. **God is a God of second chances.** He can allow us to have another chance if only we repent. Jonah was granted a second chance when he repented and confessed his wrongdoing (Jonah 3:1). The Word of the Lord came to him the second time and was given the same message he first rejected. Jonah went to Nineveh, carried out the Lord's assignment and was fruitful in the land. King Nebuchadnezzar was another person in the Bible who enjoyed the mercy of God. He was

turned to an animal for his pride but reinstated after crying for mercy and acknowledging the power of God (Daniel 4:33-37). Peter denied Jesus three times when confronted by a maiden (John 18:15-27). He misled the early apostles to their past vocation with a lot of fruitless labor (John 21). He repented and was given a second chance. You too can enjoy another opportunity from the Lord if only you will repent, acknowledge your sins and embrace Him with all your heart.

3. **Every Christian needs a vine dresser in order to bear fruit.** Even though the end of the parable was not given, I perceive it must have been a productive year. The vine dresser took his time to dig around and fertilize the tree. Digging around a tree ensures the soil is aerated, good, fertilized and also a way to protect its roots. If the root is diseased, there will be stunted growth. A vine dresser is a mentor who confronts you with the truth and has your best interest at heart. He or she digs you out to fulfill your purpose. Vine dressers speak prophetically into our lives, counsel us, correct us, guide us and bring out our best. Your vine dresser is not a parasite that competes or sucks out the nutrients you need for your growth and fruitfulness. He or she is able to root out devourers such as worms, insects, rodents and birds who pose threat to your growth and fruitfulness. He or she makes sure you are rooted and grounded in the Lord. Your vine dresser sees your blind spots and provides covering for you to make you walk in your divine destiny. I thank God for sending such people to my life in my hour of need. They have been of tremendous blessings to me.

THERE IS A NEED TO JUMP IN THE DEEP END

I have learnt that to not take a risk is risky. Many have been paralyzed with fear, unnecessary worry and anxiety which waste our time and torment us. The Israelites were in a state of fear for forty days when faced with Goliath. The emotional trauma on them was huge. David came to the scene and stumbled on the opportunity of a lifetime. Many are afraid today to step into opportunities God brings their way. Goliath was described in 1 Samuel 17:4–7 (MSG) as "a giant nearly ten feet tall stepped out from the Philistine line into the open, Goliath from Gath. He had a bronze helmet on his head and was dressed in armor, 126 pounds of it! He wore bronze shin guards and carried a bronze sword. His spear was like a fence rail, the spear tip alone weighed over fifteen pounds. His shield bearer walked ahead of him." Yet, David summoned courage (based on the foundation of God's faithfulness in his life); approached Goliath in the name of the great God and killed Goliath.

In the parable of the talents in Matthew 25, Jesus tells us about the master of a house that went on a journey and decided to give his three servants talents based on their abilities. Their master of course knew their character, attitude, motivation, personality and productivity. He also knew how much each one could handle. It was his prerogative on how he distributed the talents since he owned them. He called his servants by their names and gave one five talents, another two talents and the third was given one talent. They were all given specific instructions of trading with the talents.

The first one took risk and invested his five talents which yielded 100 percent returns (another five talents). The second one also invested his two talents by taking business risk and he also had 100 percent returns (another two talents). The third servant refused to take risk and buried the talent. I will describe him as a lazy, unmotivated, manipulative, ungrateful, ignorant, fearful, frustrated, angry and carnal person. These negative qualities are not acceptable in God's kingdom. His reply to his master (Matthew 25:24-25) when asked to give account of his stewardship reveals his malicious heart, nonchalant and spiteful attitude. His response to his master was very vicious. He was obnoxious and obsessed with having his own way. He felt rigid in his beliefs. Obviously he did not appreciate his master.

This man's other problem was his wrong perception and impression of his master and hence was destined to fail. His heart was definitely polluted and poisoned. He must have held this perception for some time. I see him as a kind of person that bore grudges. *The person you do not admire, you cannot serve.* If you don't celebrate greatness, you cannot attract greatness. It is true that *the anointing one attacks, one cannot attract.* His master diagnosed him right by saying in Matthew 25:26-27: "You wicked, lazy servant! So you knew that I harvest where I have not sown and gather where I have not scattered seed? Well then, you should have put my money on deposit with the bankers, so that when I returned I would have received it back with interest." The parable confirms God's expectation for His children and that is to bear fruit.

BLOSSOM PRINCIPLES

1. God demands fruitfulness from His children and He expects returns on His investment.

2. One of the purposes of our creation is to bear fruits and be relevant in our land.

3. It is never late for a child of God to fulfill the commandments of God on fruitfulness.

4. Our God is a God of second chances and will give you another chance if you repent.

5. God is more interested in building our character than our charisma.

6. God has a timetable for us and He expects us to bear fruit within a certain time frame.

7. Unfruitfulness is undesirable in God's kingdom.

8. Every Christian needs a vine dresser (mentor) who has their best interest at heart to confront them with the truth.

9. To not take a risk is risky.

10. If you do not celebrate greatness, you cannot attract greatness.

NOTES

I will be like the dew to Israel;
he will blossom like a lily.
Like a cedar of Lebanon he will
send down his roots.

HOSEA 14:5

EPILOGUE

I t is the responsibility of believers to blossom. God promised it and set man up for it. It is a matter of choice whether we blossom or not. There is a need for God to work in us in order for us to lay hold and walk in His promises. Man lost the power in Eden through Adam and Eve, but God has redeemed us to Himself through His only begotten Son Jesus Christ. We need to be connected to God through Jesus to reactivate the power God deposited in man from the beginning. Peter said in 2 Peter 1:3-4:

> "His divine power has given us everything we need for a godly life through our knowledge of him who called us by his own glory and goodness. Through these he has given us his very great and precious promises, so that through them you may participate in the divine nature, having escaped the corruption in the world caused by evil desires."

This power is called *Dunamis* in Greek and it is the inherent power that delivers the blessings and promises of God into our hands. Jesus warned the disciples not to start their ministry without this power that comes from the Holy Spirit's indwelling or baptism (Acts 1:8). When this power came upon the disciples in Jerusalem on the day of Pentecost, noticeable changes took place in their lives. They were emboldened, empowered, encouraged, enlightened and enriched with the creative miracles of God to blossom in the land. Every Christian needs to be filled with this power from the Holy Spirit. It is this power that releases what a Christian needs to blossom. Every Christian who wants to blossom must understand that to blossom is a function of faith, not gait and a function of grace, not race or face.

TO BLOSSOM IS A FUNCTION OF FAITH AND NOT GAIT

It is not as a result of your long legs or how fast you can be connected to man. Man will fail and only God cannot fail. Our faith should be in God and not man. The Bible tells us the arm of flesh will definitely fail. Faith is the confidence that what we hope for will actually happen; it gives us assurance about things we cannot see. Faith in God involves believing God for His promises. God has great and precious promises for us and it takes faith to obtain those promises. Faith believes in the ability and capability of God. God is able to do all things. We cannot overdraw God's account and no matter how big we think or ask, we can still not overwhelm Him with our request.

Faith in God is giving God the control of our lives no matter the circumstances we face. Faith in God makes us put God in the driver seat where we allow Him to lead and guide us. Faith conquers fear. Faith holds on to the words of God and believes His integrity as written in Ecclesiastes 3:14: "I know that everything God does will endure forever; nothing can be added to it and nothing taken from it. God does it so that people will fear him." Faith in God is an unshaken belief in the Creator and Possessor of the universe. Faith gives one the ability to not fret but to delight and trust in the Lord in all situations.

The early part of Joshua's ministry teaches us on how to increase in faith. Moses had just died and everybody was mourning the loss of a great leader. Moses was highly anointed of God – it takes anointing to command the ground to open up and swallow rebellious people in the camp of Israel (Numbers 16). As Moses' assistant, Joshua was privy to all the amazing things that happened in the ministry of Moses. Joshua was afraid to step into Moses' shoes and more so, there was a Jordan River to cross. He stood paralyzed with overwhelming emotions like the rest of Israelites. The Lord spoke to the spirit of Joshua and empowered him. His faith was stirred up and he embraced the mantle of leadership. God told Joshua to be strong and courageous. It was repeated thrice and the word of faith resonated in his mind. We receive this virtue in place of fear when we call to remembrance the mighty move of God in our lives or around us.

Like Joshua, the young Timothy was encouraged to stir up the gift of God in him and to remember the faith of his grandmother and mother. Precious reminders of God's miracles in our lives will help lift up our faith to conquer today or tomorrow's challenges.

God challenged Joshua to meditate on His word (Joshua 1:8). The Word of God has a way of perfecting our faith. Romans 10:17 (NKJV) says "So then faith comes by hearing, and hearing by the word of God." There is power in the Word. Every effort must be made to read, hear, memorize, meditate and obey the Word of God. The Word is Jesus (John 1:1) and the Word has the ability to create something from nothing and turn the ordinary to extraordinary.

Through the Word of God, a chaotic and void world was turned around and the beautiful work of God's masterpiece came into being. Through the Word, the dead Lazarus was also called forth to life and the ordinary water at Cana of Galilee was turned to a tasteful wine.

We can increase in faith by serving God. Joshua stepped out to serve God and lead the Israelites. His faith in God increased through his service. By faith, he led the Israelites across the Jordan River; pulled down the wall of Jericho without a bulldozer or bomb and made the moon and sun stand still by merely speaking. As a result of his experience, Joshua emphasized the importance of serving God.

Joshua 24:14-15
"Now fear the LORD and serve him with all faithfulness. Throw away the gods your ancestors worshiped beyond the Euphrates River and in Egypt, and serve the LORD. But if serving the LORD seems undesirable to you, then choose for yourselves this day whom you will serve, whether the gods your ancestors served beyond the Euphrates, or the gods of the Amorites, in whose land you are living. But as for me and my household, we will serve the LORD."

TO BLOSSOM, IS A FUNCTION OF GRACE AND NOT RACE OR FACE

It is not about your look or color. Grace is what makes every lily to blossom (Hosea 14:5). Grace is the undeserved favor of God. It cannot be earned. Grace enriches, empowers and enlightens. Grace makes the race of life easy and exciting. Grace brings new life and power on a platter of gold. God's grace on Daniel made him blossom in Babylon. The grace of God on Esther added color, beauty and favor to her life and transformed her from a servant to a beautiful queen. Grace supersedes our efforts and replaces labor with favor. It covers our small and big deficiencies. Ecclesiastes 9:11 says: "The race is not to the swift or the battle to the strong, nor does food come to the wise or wealth to the brilliant or favor to the learned; but time and chance happen to them all." Grace makes the difference and puts an end to struggle and striving. Grace brings increase, riches and abundance from our loving father. We increase in grace by living a life of holiness (Romans 6:1-2) and humbling ourselves before God (James 4:6). God will always give grace if we cry to Him. He always enjoins us to come boldly to His throne of grace (Hebrews 4:16).

With Grace, anything that hinders growth can be removed without stress. Grace removes the act of omission and commission that can prevent you from blossoming. With grace, great advancement and exploits are possible when circumstances around you are stating the opposite. Grace will turn a hard ground to a soft and fertile soil that will bring forth abundant harvest. When a Christian combines faith and grace, he or she will bring forth extraordinary riches, uncommon blessings or wealth and supernatural product. The source of grace and faith is Jesus. To blossom, we need to be connected to Jesus. We must have Him as our personal Lord and Savior.

As you blossom in life, you need to watch out for the following:

Beware of Critics. The purpose of critics is to discourage, demoralize, distract and change you. Do not allow people who are going nowhere to distract you from reaching your goals. Nehemiah faced his own critics and made a profound statement that the critics will not chase him out of his divine assignment (Nehemiah 6:11).

Watch out for false hopes. Some associations are not necessary but simply clog your wheel of progress. There are lots of imposters today who deceive and manipulate with their sugar-coated tongues. Some relationships tear up our faith instead of building it. Dissociate from friends who are not adding value to your life.

BLOSSOM · OLAYINKA DADA M.D.

Ignorance kills faster than cancer today. Hosea 4:6 says "My people are destroyed for lack of knowledge." Ignorance will rob us of God's eternal treasure. We conquer ignorance by seeking knowledge (2 Timothy 2:15). Study goes beyond mere reading; it involves careful examination, investigation, application and practice of knowledge.

Beware of sycophants. It is quite unfortunate that there are lots of flatterers in the church today who come with their "sir" or "ma" greetings. They say something and do something entirely different. They are hypocritical and possess stubborn hearts. Jesus addressed this spirit in Matthew 21:28-31. They portray themselves as if they are spiritual but with underlying agenda for position, power and fame. It takes discernment to be able to recognize and place them appropriately.

Do not forget God, our Source. Never make your wealth the center of your life. Look to God and serve Him. Never grumble as God unfolds the events of your life because grumbling is an expression of unbelief and ingratitude. Grumbling disconnects you from God. When you are disconnected you lack power. Grumbling makes you stink in the sight of God. A grumbler cannot live long. They die prematurely. The Bible says in Proverbs 18:21 that "death and life are in the power of tongue; they that love it shall eat the fruit thereof."

God is worthy of our praise at all times.

BLOSSOM PRINCIPLES

1. Blossoming is a function of faith and not gait.

2. Faith in God is an unshaken belief in the Creator and Possessor of the universe.

3. Precious reminders of God's mighty moves in our lives should be replayed to conquer today's challenges.

4. Blossoming is a function of grace and not race.

5. Grace makes the journey to blossoming easy and exciting.

6. Beware of the tactics of critics. Don't let them change you.

7. Seek knowledge; we conquer ignorance by seeking knowledge.

8. There is power in the spoken word. Watch your words. Learn to speak life to your situations.

Catch all the foxes, those little foxes,
before they ruin the vineyard of love,
for the grapevines are blossoming!

SONG OF SOLOMON 2:15 NLT

ACKNOWLEDGEMENTS

I give glory to God for the successful completion of this book. At a point it seemed like a herculean task and the Lord showed up again in my life and ministry. This book is a testament of His great blessings upon my life.

Words cannot express my profound love and appreciation to my father and mother in the Lord, Pastor and Pastor (Mrs.) Adeboye. I am grateful for their prayers, impartation, love and direction.

I salute the unequivocal love of all my siblings. I love you all and pray for more of His grace in our family.

My editor really challenged me this time to bring out my best for this work. I am extremely grateful for your style and attention to details.

I say a big thank you to my destiny partners: Pastors Bode and Kemi Akindele, Pastors Benjamin and Belinda Enoma. You have all given me useful recommendations in getting the work done.

My appreciation goes to all my spiritual children worldwide and members of *Restoration House Hamilton*. Thank you.

My special appreciation goes to my mentors: Dr. Myles Munroe, for inspiring me to continue to fulfill my purpose and for writing the foreword; Dr. Sam Chand and Rev. George Adegboye for their spiritual guidance.

I am also grateful to The Redeemed Christian Church of God North American (RCCGNA) Coordinators, Provincial Pastors and Pastor James Fadele, Chairman RCCGNA whose advice, prayers and love have always encouraged me.

I thank the Most High God for my loving wife, Oluwatoyin Abimbola for being the virtuous woman described in Proverbs 31. You are really a jewel of inestimable value and I appreciate your love. May God increase you more and more.

OTHER RESOURCES BY
DR. OLAYINKA DADA

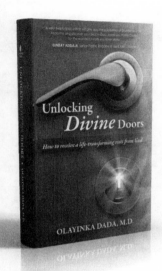

Unlocking Divine Doors:

How to receive a life-transforming
visit from God

The Highest Common Factor:

Understanding the grace phenomenon

www.yinkadada.com

NOTES

NOTES

NOTES

NOTES